The Art, Science, and Spirituality
of the Female Orgasm

The Art, Science, and Spirituality of the Female Orgasm

NICOLE DAEDONE

TERESA DIAZ, MD

soulmaker | PRESS

soulmakerpress.com
Santa Rosa, California

ISBN: 978-1-961064-33-1 (Paperback)
ISBN: 978-1-961064-34-8 (eBook)

Library of Congress Catalog Number: 2025907216

For G.
Real heroes do exist

—Nicole

Contents

Introduction

For centuries, the female orgasm has been misunderstood, diminished, and even feared. Stripped of its true meaning, it has been reduced to a fleeting peak—a bonus, a mystery, or something to be chased and achieved. Yet orgasm is far more than a moment. It is a state of being, an ongoing current that, when understood and cultivated, has the power to transform not just sex, but life itself.

This book is an invitation to reclaim that power.

Science is only beginning to catch up to what women have known in their bones: Orgasm is not simply a function of pleasure but a vital force that shapes the mind, body, and spirit. It influences our creativity, emotional well-being, health, and even the way we move through the world. When women are disconnected from their full orgasmic nature, they are cut off from a vast wellspring of vitality, often without realizing it.

If you have ever sensed that something is missing in the way sexuality is framed, you are not alone. If you have ever felt a deep knowing that there must be more—more depth, more connection, more aliveness—you are not mistaken. This book presents a radical shift in how we understand orgasm: not as an endpoint, but as an entryway into an expansive, sustained state of being.

The Problem We Face

The suppression of female sexuality is one of the most pervasive and damaging forms of control—so embedded in culture, it often goes unnoticed. Women have been conditioned to feel shame about their desire, to approach sex as a performance rather than an expression of self, to believe their pleasure is secondary or excessive. Many have internalized the message that there is something dangerous, overwhelming, or even wrong about their own erotic nature.

This conditioning does not simply live in the mind—it embeds itself in the body. It numbs sensation, creates disconnection, and manifests in everything from emotional exhaustion to chronic stress to physical illness. Mainstream approaches to sexual health rarely address this deeper reality, leaving many women with an unspoken, unshakable feeling of incompleteness.

But there is a way back.

The Life That Becomes Possible

When you step into the full force of your orgasmic nature—not as an isolated burst, but as a continuous state—you awaken something extraordinary. You become more attuned to your body, more emotionally resilient, more deeply present in every moment of your life. Research shows that embracing pleasure and releasing shame has measurable effects: reducing stress, improving immune function, balancing hormones, and even accelerating physical healing.

Beyond the physiological, the shift is profound:

- **Emotional Aliveness:** An orgasmic life cultivates self-awareness, authenticity, and the capacity for deeper joy.

- **Physical Vitality:** The body thrives when it is fully inhabited, when sensation is welcomed rather than feared.
- **Deeper Intimacy:** A woman who owns her erotic power moves differently in relationships. She is able to connect without grasping, to give without depletion.
- **Spiritual Expansion:** Orgasm is a portal into presence, a direct experience of connection with oneself, others, and life itself.

This book is a reclamation. Of pleasure. Of truth. Of the full, undiluted force of female erotic power.

What awaits is a fuller, richer, more electrifying life.

About the Authors

Nicole Daedone is a pioneering teacher and thought leader in the realms of human consciousness, relationships, and sexuality. Her work has been featured in major publications, and her TEDx talk on Orgasmic Meditation (OM) has reached a global audience. At the core of her life's work is a singular vision: revealing the untapped potential of human connection. Her understanding of orgasm as a force for deep transformation is central to that mission.

Dr. Teresa Diaz is a practicing OB/GYN and a member of The Institute for Functional Medicine. Through her years in medicine, she has witnessed firsthand how sexual disconnection contributes to illness, stress, and emotional depletion. Her work bridges modern science with ancient wisdom, illuminating the body's profound capacity for healing through conscious embodiment and pleasure. Dr. Diaz's own journey—from growing up in a culture that suppressed her power to becoming an

OM practitioner—reflects her unwavering belief that unlocking our innate vitality can reshape not only our health but our entire lives.

Throughout this book, you'll find sections written by Dr. Diaz, offering a medical lens on orgasm's far-reaching impact—how it supports physical well-being, emotional resilience, and even the healing of deep-seated trauma.

An Invitation to Transformation

This book is not about better sex—though that could be a by-product. It is about breaking the cycle of shame and misinformation that has kept women from fully inhabiting their own bodies. It is about tapping into the quiet, continuous current of orgasmic energy that moves beneath the surface of daily life. It is about reclaiming pleasure—not as an indulgence, but as a pathway to deep fulfillment, richer relationships, and an inherent sense of wholeness.

If you have ever questioned whether there is more to orgasm—and more to yourself—than you have been taught to believe, you are right. Together, Nicole Daedone and Dr. Teresa Diaz will guide you toward a new understanding: Orgasm is not a brief release, but an ongoing experience of aliveness. And when you embrace it fully, it opens a door—not just to a new relationship with your body, but to an entirely different way of being.

Read on with an open mind, a curious heart, and a willingness to rediscover what has always been yours. Your life will be infinitely richer for it.

Let's begin.

CHAPTER 1

Redefining Orgasm

It begins as a slight trembling sensation, like water over stone, and a sense of something even bigger beneath the rippling surface. The molecules below slowly begin their dance. A soft building flow that begins to gather and rise, the prick of magnetism, a purring motor, an electric current running through the body. And suddenly a sense of rising up, an ascent into rarefied air, a sharp inhalation and up, up, up, the tipping point to go over, the welling and the initial flood, the momentum taking you higher into an entirely new space. Beyond surrender, voluntary or involuntary. The sense of self falls into the sweeping river, and there is no separation between the coursing molecules, the flashes of light and darkness, no thought or will or action in the way that a waterfall has no other option but to cascade and roar, froth and churn. A place unknown, a glimpse into the bellow of the universe. Hollowing, emptying, filling.

Nothing guards the door. This is beyond control, beyond return. You are lit up with potential and everything is possible—you are free.

This is the essence of orgasm, when we feel most truly ourselves and our lives feel most entirely lived. But instead, so many women keep their orgasmic potential at an arm's length. Speak to a woman about her orgasm and she might flush and smile or toss out a joke to diffuse the tension. Some women blush and shrink in their chair, embarrassed to talk about something so personal! Others might flash a furrowed brow or pained expression and change the subject.

Anything that evokes sex can be fraught, because entangled with sex are myriad memories, projections, and expectations. For no small number of women, sex is a performance, or a chore. It may evoke shame, or blame— *I can't get off* or *he can't get me off*. Just consider that expression for a moment—to *get off*. For many, sex can end up boiling down to an almost choreographed series of motions and positions, all in an effort to temporarily alter our state, to get out of our minds and all of the constant worrying and judging that happens inside them.

Ecstasy doesn't share space, so in those moments when we're truly overtaken, it feels like relief. There's a sense of weightlessness as all of our mental burdens dissolve into bliss. And then we return. Back to the dishes. Back to our career. Back to our lackluster relationships.

Maybe the word "orgasm" conjures up ideas from *Fifty Shades of Grey*, or lights off in the missionary position, or fantasies of your gym trainer and what you'd like him to do to you if the two of you were ever alone. But none of that is orgasm. At least, it's not all that orgasm can be, and it won't take you to the places that *real* orgasm can take you. When I say *real orgasm*, I'm talking about full, ongoing access to your sexuality—to the source of female power.

When I asked a group of women, "Why is women's sexuality powerful?" I got some very revealing answers:

"Because it is ours to do whatever we want with."

"Because every institution throughout time, throughout history, has tried to suppress it."

"Because when I feel fulfilled and happy, I'm spreading that energy to everyone."

"Because it brings life and connection."

"Because it governs all of society around us."

"Because women who embrace their sexuality are healthier."

"Because it creates life."

"Because, when a woman is connected to her own sexuality, she can do anything."

We know inherently that there is a power in women's sexuality, and yet most of how we think of sex and express it in our culture is oriented around men and their desire and ideas of sex. Male pleasure is taken as a given, while female enjoyment of sex, when it happens, is thought of as a bonus. With that perspective of sex, it's not surprising that we assume men are the initiators, while women are passive or even resistant to sex. There are so many obstacles and dangers in the way of a woman expressing her sexuality that few even venture to explore it fully, and those who do are branded sluts, whores, "used up," immodest, immoral, temptress, or even witch. There's a long history to the fear and repression of women's sexuality that still exists in the cultural programming today and all the way into our own bodies.

If we were to tap into the very essence of feminine sexuality, *orgasm*—and I mean that in a different way than we've come to think of it—we would discover an entirely new perspective to women's sexuality, arousal, and power. Out there in the world, the term orgasm is usually used to refer to *sexual climax*, just the *peak* of sensation before things come back down. That may be the moment the power of our orgasm is so activated that it takes hold of our awareness and our bodies—loudly or quietly, in a burst or a slow-rolling wave, rising and crashing over us before slipping back under the surface. But under the surface, orgasm flows through us, shaping our desires and guiding us through the sensations and experience of our life.

Orgasm extends far beyond the conventional understanding of a fleeting sexual climax. In mainstream discourse, orgasm is often reduced to the peak of physical pleasure—a brief, localized event that fades quickly. However, in the framework of Eros, orgasm is an ongoing flow of vital and creative energy that permeates all aspects of life.

True orgasm is not just a moment of release, but a continuous state of being, an open channel of sensation and connection to the deeper forces of existence. It is the current that shapes our desires and fuels our power, guiding our experience of life itself. Climax is merely a glimpse of this expansive energy, like the tip of an iceberg, while the true depth of orgasm resides beneath the surface, flowing through us at all times.

To live in orgasm means to embrace this state as a way of engaging with the world—one of receptivity, surrender, flow, and deep attunement to the present moment. It is a practice of opening fully to what arises, whether pleasure or pain, without suppression or avoidance. This redefinition invites us to reclaim orgasm not just as a sexual event, but as a transformative power that can shape our lives, our relationships, and our connection to all that is.

That is what I am referring to when I say orgasm. Climax is just the tip of the iceberg, a window that is ready to draw us down into the depths, our deepest nature, our power and freedom. Orgasm is the nexus that connects us to the whole of our lives, our bodies, and the world around us. I proudly believe that female orgasm is the most powerful force on the planet. If all our orgasm means to us is that passing flash of contractions followed by sleepy relief, then we reduce what is possible for our orgasm to some anatomical byproduct of men's reproductive sexual reflex and our female bodies just to baby factories.

Climax is a brief, intense physiological event characterized by a peak of sensation, followed by an abrupt release of built-up tension. Unlike orgasm, which is understood as an ongoing state of expanded awareness, creativity, and erotic flow, climax is a short-lived discharge that restores homeostasis but does not sustain or deepen the erotic experience.

Most people in our culture are conditioned for "habituated climax"—a momentary burst of pleasure that often leaves them feeling depleted rather than fulfilled. This kind of climax is driven by a need for relief, a mechanical reaction to tension rather than an embodied engagement with sensation. In contrast, non-habituated climax allows for a more fluid experience where energy is not simply expelled but transformed, leading to deeper states of erotic consciousness.

> While climax is often mistaken for the full experience of orgasm, it is merely a surface-level event—akin to a lightning bolt that briefly illuminates the sky, whereas orgasm is the ongoing storm of sensation and energy moving through the body.

Deep down, we know there's more to our orgasm than just that—and we've tried to reach that "more" in so many ways. We've tried to "achieve" our orgasm with all kinds of toys and tips from the covers of *Cosmopolitan,* or given up on all that to just get what satisfaction we may from our job or family, being a good woman inside a narrow, prescribed life, skirting the surface of what we sense is possible.

Women carry a hidden hunger, a force so vast it could remake the world if only we dared to unleash it. Only, it doesn't gnaw in the stomach; it thrums as anxiety, hums as stress, sharpens into the constant vigilance we've been taught to mistake for survival.

It takes root quietly, disguising itself so that instead of reaching for what we need, we learn to name it something else: worry, neuroses, a personal failing. We've been trained to suppress it, to choke it back the way we've been taught to temper our appetite for food. And yet, the hunger remains.

It is the hunger for an unleashing of our creative erotic force: *orgasm.* The untapped current of life itself.

To name it is an act of rebellion. To feel it fully is an act of reclamation. And to unleash it is to finally, undeniably, rise. Because this hunger is not just ours, it is the world's—waiting for us to feed it, to let it burn through everything false and leave only what is true.

And when we do, the world will never be the same.

Opening to Freedom

True orgasm is like that moment just before climax, when everything in the world feels lit up with potential and all things seem possible. When we can orient to all of life from orgasm, all things truly are possible. This is what it means to be free.

"Why do you stay in prison, when the door is so wide open?"[1] That's the question the mystical poet Rumi posed, and that's what I want to ask you. You certainly don't owe me any answers or explanations—it's a question to answer for yourself. "Why am I holding myself back? Why am I keeping myself from connecting with my power?" We could step through the doorway into bliss, into the experience and depth of orgasm, but we hold ourselves back. There is no one else who could cross that threshold; the power is ours alone. As Rumi goes on to write, "The entrance door to the sanctuary is inside you."

Before you recoil, and before you start talking about men and the patriarchy, let's stop and strip away all of that deflection, all the stories about how it's men who keep us down—how they hoard all of the goods for themselves and how they have to share their power in order for us to have any. I understand. I studied women's studies and semantics at University of California San Francisco in the 1990s, and so I spent *a lot* of time on that particular soapbox, decrying all of the injustices that women suffer at the hands of men. It was convenient to believe, exceptionally effective at shielding me from my own power. From my own *desire* for power.

Take a moment to envision everything inside of you that feels restricted, constricted, held back, suppressed, compressed, repressed, or muted.

Chances are, there's a lot there. That's the case for most

1. Coleman Barks, *The Essential Rumi* (Castle Books, 1997), 3.

women. Over the years, somewhere inside you, a massive dam has been constructed and it's holding you back. Who built it? We may tell ourselves society, or simply men, built it. But again, that's a bit of a cop-out. Whoever is responsible for building these walls, you've been the one keeping up the maintenance, reinforcing them against the ever-rising tide that swells within you, then pools.

This stagnant lake trapped inside you yearns to flow with your vitality, your thriving, your joy.

Some part of you feels hopeless, believing you will always be kept separate from it. "That's life!" a bitter and listless voice declares, but it doesn't have to be.

One thing has the power to burst that dam. To dislodge the blockage and set the river running. It is your sexuality.

So, why is orgasm so mind-blowing? As the poet and feminist Audre Lorde put it, "The erotic is a resource within each of us that lies in a deeply female and spiritual plane, firmly rooted in the power of our unexpressed or unrecognized feeling." Drop into the experience at the edge of climax—the raw heat that dissolves all edges and boundaries, the expression of energy that crackles through every detail and surface, your experience of the totality of that moment free of the finite limitations of me and not-me, real and unreal. Feel it in your body, feel what's there, and what's not. What dissolves, and what becomes evident in its absence. Our goal is to live all of life from that reality, at that level of awareness, that pristine sensitivity. It is possible, it is beautiful, it is challenging, and it is worth it.

When sexual energy floods the body, the consciousness is soaked in what it truly desires, satisfying every concern or craving of the thinking brain. In this moment, the part of us that's so obsessed with incessant evaluation and judgment is silenced in awe. Immersed in orgasm, the mind can recognize that all its creations, entire cultures of art and poetry and architecture, are all in devotion, reaching for this. Beyond the ritual and solemnity of masculine spirituality, this is the ecstatic, rapturous, direct and unmediated experience of feminine spirituality. This is the experience we reach for through our sexuality and in so many other ways—and that men try to reach through us. Our direct access to the complete experience of orgasm is the core of our power.

The truth is that women have a full-body autoimmune response to the idea of claiming their own power. Not to all power, but to feminine power and our own orgasm, which is at the very center of it. After all, we've been taught that to get ahead in the world or to master life, we must play the man's game, and so it's masculine power we've learned to wield in the world. But there's another game—one we are quite literally built to play as it involves owning and inhabiting our own power.

Feminine power is rooted in what makes us unique as women. Our bodies are built to take in and create; we are uniquely sensitive to our bodies, others, and our surroundings. Our beings are sexual, sensual, and evocative. We birth life into the world, and so we understand the interconnections between people at a deep and intimate level that men may not recognize. Woman is the gateway to the feminine plane, the ground of fertility, and our power exists at this level. When we claim this ground, it becomes the source of our power. When we allow our landscape of desires and emotions to express and, just as openly, draw in the full experience offered back to us by the world, we discover the power we've eschewed for so long.

We've mistaken power for force. Power exists as a whole, a field like gravity—it *creates* without requiring energy from any external source. On the other hand, force is what acts on those creations, as one bumps into the next and things are built or taken apart, by force and counterforce. Masculine power follows the rules of force. Men love to manufacture, to debate the merits of this versus that, to take things apart and figure out how they work, the internal forces acting on each other. We've seen all kinds of scientific experiments that show this divide even as young as newborns—boys often are more interested in things and systems, while girls typically are more interested in people, empathy, and relationships. These relational qualities are native to how women engage with the world. They are the channels through which we express power and how we are nourished. But, they've become increasingly foreign in a world where women expect themselves to do everything a man can do, while cut off from their own source of power.

Feminine power is the innate ability to attract, receive, and transform. It is the infinite and self-generating force that uplifts and creates. Unlike masculine power, which operates through production and control, feminine power is autotelic—fulfilling in itself—and unconditional, existing beyond external circumstances.

A woman in her power does not need to dominate or assert herself aggressively; she moves the world around her simply by being in full presence. She influences through Call—the ability to summon and guide others through resonance rather than demand. Feminine power is deeply connected to the body and is rooted in interdependence rather than separation.

This power is often misunderstood or repressed, leading to burnout, disconnection, or the mistaken belief that force is required to succeed in a masculine-driven world. However, when cultivated, feminine power allows for effortless creation, optionality, and wisdom. It is not passive but deeply active in its ability to inspire and bring forth transformation.

In its everyday manifestations, this looks like burnout. Fatigue. Depression. Lethargy. Interpersonal friction. Judgment. Physical autoimmune issues. But these are just some of the many cloaks worn by one entity—women's disconnection from ourselves and a feminine expression of power. Not just a passive disconnection, but for many an outright aversion to anything resembling a woman's true power and to the responsibilities that come with wielding it. Because that's what is required to truly harness this power. You must relinquish the option of pretending to be weak or unimportant. No more hiding.

For many of us, that's terrifying. After all, it's for good reason we hide. We all know what happens to women who inhabit female power. They are stoned, beheaded, burned at the stake. They are ridiculed, reviled, canceled. We've seen it done to others, it's done to us, and we do it to one another. Because when even one woman wields her power, it dispels the myth of women's powerlessness and all the secondary benefits we gain from that—the protection of men, freedom from responsibility, freedom from choice and agency. These are the freedoms of dependency, the freedoms enjoyed by children. That is the addiction we have developed, hiding in the shadow of our choice to an addiction we have cocreated with the help of men and their own addiction to domination and control. As a result, we make ourselves small out of a strategy of survival, but certainly not of flourishing.

We have learned to make ourselves appear weak, casting ourselves as victims and blaming others when we lack what we want, when we feel empty or exhausted. We may even resent our own womanhood and its perceived burdens.

We have played the role of a princess, reluctant to accept the worldly responsibilities of a queen. These are the responsibilities of motherhood—to accept the mantle as the provider not just for another living being, but for all beings. To be that important, that powerful, that consequential can feel overwhelming; to know that one's role cannot be filled in the exact same way by any other person on the planet. For a woman to accept this brand of power means stepping into the larger version of herself and being accountable for the influence she wields. A princess can feign frailty and fragility. She can stay locked in a tower awaiting rescue. But a queen has no such luxury. She must leave behind the indulgences of adolescence. As she assumes the throne, she swears her life to her country, pledging to inhabit her role with both fierceness and grace for the good of all. We can call this *sacrifice*, but offered willingly, it is *devotion*.

To be sure, the world is not supportive of mothers, and it certainly does not welcome reigning queens, but we need not blame men for this, nor rely on them to change these or any of our other circumstances. I am not saying your misery, your dissatisfaction, your boredom, or your exhaustion are your fault. They are not. They are simply a byproduct of a distorted, emaciated approach to life. We've bought into a stunted perception of how women should walk through the world, devoid of our own independence, the weaker other half of men. We can change that perception. We can learn to take the brave step *inward* and embrace our own significance. To do that, we must *want* to be free, *want* to embody the feminine power available to us, embracing the power of Call.

Call is the subtle yet powerful ability to attract and influence people or situations, without force. It is a fundamental expression of feminine power—an unseen yet deeply felt energy that shapes the world by drawing others in. Unlike the masculine form of power, which often seeks to control through effort and domination, Call operates through resonance and presence.

Call is not about manipulation or coercion; it is the natural emanation of a woman fully connected to herself. It flows from a place of self-possession, where a woman is neither grasping for attention nor shrinking from it but instead radiating a magnetic presence. This energy can manifest as an almost instinctual ability to shift the emotional and energetic states of those around her, influencing them without the need for direct action.

When a woman embodies Call, she transmits a clear, directed signal—one that can inspire others and move them toward their highest potential. It is the force behind a glance that shifts the mood of a room, a voice that commands attention without raising in volume, and a presence that lingers long after she has left. It is the capacity to affect change not by pushing, but by being.

If you watch a novice flamenco dancer, the movements are beautiful and emphatic—loud and attention-grabbing. The dancer's power comes from force. But watching a more seasoned artist, their movements are subtle yet far more impactful; the movement of a finger, the turning of a wrist, or the smallest of glances is mesmerizing. The dancer has *duende*—the ability to move another human being, to draw them forward with consciously directed energy. This is Call. It is *your* ability to move mountains with little to no effort. When we own our Call, we shift from viewing life as something that happens to us to recognizing ourselves as the originators of our experience.

Call is not only the realm of seasoned dancers, it is every woman's birthright. It is yours to claim. This is a woman's power to wield.

It's Teresa here. Throughout the book you'll see my stories and insights set off in these gray boxes.

As a child, then a young woman growing up in New York, we were always being catcalled. Men—even the kids in junior high school—were grabbing my breasts, grabbing my butt. That's how they did it. Over time it began to be normal to us that men did that, that boys did that; nobody stopped them. I was also sexually abused by many of the men and boys around me, so with all of that trauma, I didn't want male attention. I hid from it. I put on layers both literally and figuratively to shield myself from this world of sex and sexuality. I've seen similar behavior among many of my patients, too. Sexuality and being a woman feel like a burden. There's a lot we avoid or put up with as a result. I remember as a child, if I walked in front of a man I would try not to move my body too much so I didn't call attention to myself. Lots of us go through our entire lives like that.

As women moving through the world, we frame much of the attention we get as negative. Through the lens of orgasm, we can see it as *unskillful*. People are responding to this pull we have, this appeal, in these clunky and aggressive ways. They don't know how to handle the energy they're feeling, and we don't know how to handle their unskillful response, so we hide. We armor up. Or some of us try to turn the tables and use that energy of sex to be in control—to be in power. To be the dominator instead of the dominated. Instead, we need to learn how to wield this power and handle what it creates skillfully. Artfully. Playfully. So we can enjoy what it is to be a woman, and do something positive with it—positive for ourselves and others. We can start to move through the world in a way that's more grounded in the body. That's how we can move out of a space of victimhood and start to channel our power.

As a physician who practices Orgasmic Meditation (OM), I sometimes ask a patient to drop into her body and put her attention on her genitals. When she does that, the entire conversation changes. It's as though I am talking to an entirely different part of them. The conversation suddenly has depth and authenticity. We can all learn to move and to relate from this space.

The path of orgasm has us move from our heads into our bodies. It's not that the mind can't also be beautiful, it's that our culture is completely biased toward it. We live in our heads. Half the time we don't even feel our emotions, we think them. And when our thoughts die down, when we're not *thinking hard*, we believe there's a kind of stupidity that takes over. But the exact opposite is true. Instead, when the chatter quiets, the path becomes clear for a deeper, truer wisdom to emerge.

Flow is the seamless movement with the current of existence, where resistance dissolves and one becomes fully immersed in the present moment. Psychologist Mihaly Csikszentmihalyi coined the term flow to describe a state of complete absorption in an experience.

In contrast to striving or controlling, flow is about attunement—listening to life's signals and responding with trust. It does not mean everything is easy or without challenge; rather, it means that everything feels *right* because we accept and engage with what arises, without constriction.

When we live in orgasm, we do not force experiences but instead allow sensation and connection to guide us—flow. Just as in Orgasmic Meditation, where a stroke follows the body's natural rhythms rather than imposing an agenda, living in flow means embracing the unfolding of life with openness and presence. It is through this state that we access our deepest vitality, creativity, and joy.

As Buddhist teacher Willa Blythe Baker explains, we're fixated on the idea of transcending our bodies. We believe enlightenment involves moving *up* toward the head. She writes, "Would that be any surprise given we are taught from a young age that our thinking mind will solve our problems? . . . But when we move vertically into the headspace, we tend to lose our thread of present-moment experience."[2]

To fully expand our consciousness necessarily includes the body. After all, when do most of us experience this total presence? In the experience of orgasm. When we are in this body-

2. Willa Blythe Baker, *The Wakeful Body: Somatic Mindfulness as a Path to Freedom* (Shambala, 2021)

based, fully activated, and yet fully released state, all of our obsession with self and other fades, along with our worries and preoccupations. The criticism, the self-blame, the comparison and concern—all of it gone. Interestingly, these are all of the things that we think have power over us; that we think we cannot control. And yet, *poof!* They've disappeared. So clearly something's off about our calculus.

In those precious moments, there is only the absolute, crystal clarity of presence. Of oneness—that awareness of complete connection with life and a sense of being in flow with all that is. It is a merging with our environment, and in this merging, we experience true intimacy, not just with a partner or even ourselves, but with all that is. It is the big-L Love. Unconditional and perfect.

So, we know we are capable of feeling that freedom and that intimacy. *Why*, then, do we experience them in these moments? *How* is it that we are freed from our perceptual prison and connected to something so much bigger?

We feel this because, as Baker explains, though we often seek presence outside of ourselves, "the body is naturally awake, in touch with the vividness and feeling of moment-by-moment experience. The body dwells in the here and now."

For most of us, it is only in these moments of sexual ecstasy that the body becomes a portal to full presence. Yet there is another body-based practice that can enable us to not just glimpse wakefulness but live in wakefulness.

Ah, but *hic sunt dracones*—here there be dragons.

Opening to Power

In the time before the world had been extensively explored and the boundaries of islands and continents were unknown, cartographers drew the boundaries they knew of. Then, beyond that, "Here be dragons." They painted oceans inhabited by sea creatures to denote *terra incognita*: unexplored territory where anything may exist—including terrifying mythical creatures. In many ways, this is how society has drawn women's bodies. A map of landmarks and organs named after the male physicians and anatomists who "discovered" them, and beyond that . . . who knows? There is something inherently mystical and inherently terrifying about a woman's unexplored territories. But you know what they say—the dragon guards the treasure.

It is in women's sexuality that our true power lies. Feminine power is based in vision and Call, evoking from the absence and nurturing that into being. If it feels vulnerable, that's because it is. As the artist Jenny Holzer described, "It's an extraordinary feeling when parts of your body are touched for the first time. I'm thinking of the sensations from sex and surgery." Our sex is the thinnest membrane between the rough, three-dimensional world and the realm of creation seeking to express through us. This is likely a different kind of sex than we're used to having.

What I'm talking about is accessing your vitality, consistently and totally unencumbered by the demands of performative sex oriented around the demands of men and their enjoyment. Since women have given up ownership, sex has been largely defined by men's priorities. Don't get me wrong—that kind of sex can be fun, but it might not be the key that unlocks the door to your full aliveness. In fact, the sexuality I'm talking about doesn't need a key at all, because I'm talking about blowing the door completely off its hinges. To live immersed in the erotic, a way of being where you live and breathe life's energy—and it lives and breathes you.

Simple, but not easy. In fact, contemplating such a shift can feel downright terrifying. *Access my own power? Thanks, but I'll pass.*

The fact is, women have a complex relationship with sex and with orgasm because we have a complex relationship with our power. Sexuality and power are so inextricably intertwined that our hang-ups and misperceptions around orgasm by extension thwart our ability to access and wield true power. These dysfunctions are reinforced by a culture steeped in the idea that women and the feminine are defective. At our best, what's native to us is still considered inferior to the masculine way of things. But truly, it is women's power that can set the world right side up.

Perhaps you're reluctant to believe that what I'm describing is possible. After all, if what I'm saying is true, we'd know about it by now, right? How is this different from what gets splashed over the cover of every women's magazine? Indeed, what I'm about to share with you in this book *isn't* entirely new; this knowledge goes back quite literally to ancient times. But it has, like so much other information that would serve to liberate us, gone into hiding.

In her book, *When God Was a Woman*, feminist theologist Merlin Stone examines how ancient societies revered female deities and how this veneration influenced women's roles, particularly in sexuality. She discusses the *qadishtu*—"sacred priestesses" who engaged in sexual rites as a form of worship and communion with the Goddess. These priestesses held autonomy over their sexuality, operating outside the constraints of monogamy, and their sexual activities were conducted on their own terms.

As men sought to establish patrilineal inheritance, there was a deliberate effort to suppress these practices and diminish the role of women. By controlling women's sexuality, men could ensure the legitimacy of their offspring and maintain property and lineage through the male line. This shift led to the marginalization of goddess worship and the erosion of women's sexual autonomy, as patriarchal religions and phallocentric societal structures—including sexual customs—worked to subordinate women and their roles.

The suppression of goddess-centered religions and the usurpation of women's sexual autonomy were instrumental in the development of patriarchal societies. This transformation not only altered religious practices but also redefined women's status and power to this day and even the history of that time has been recast by men—female-centric spiritual practices are pronounced "fertility cults," and those sacred priestesses, the *qadishtu*, are referred to simply as the "temple prostitutes," or at best, the "sacred whores." The masculine lens is so dominant in our culture, we often mistake their narrative as "just the way things are."

But this spirituality, this access to the mystical, remains built into the cells of our bodies. We know the dragon, but we've been afraid to dance with it, to embrace our sexuality as the true source of our power. Instead, we hide and protest that men only see us as *sexual objects* (even though every Halloween, we're grabbing for garters and stilettos).

You know all of this is true—because you can *feel* it. It may seem like an affront to our modern, rational minds, but your deeper senses that still roam free within you, undomesticated and craving truth, know it. If you tune in to *this* wild, natural self—this animal-self, this tree-self with tendril roots reaching deep into the loamy ground—you will feel the resonance arising from within that knows this simply as truth. There *is* a way to optimize and unleash your sexual power, and it will lead to your emergence as a fully embodied woman.

What I'm offering you is freedom from the struggle. An end to the searching. The opportunity to claim who you really are . . . as terrifying as that may sound. It starts by shifting your understanding of orgasm from a momentary pleasure to achieve, to orgasm as a sustained state of vivid clarity from which you live and operate. That is the promise: to leave behind the depression, the burnout, the fragility, resentment, and exhaustion, and the chronic issues and patterns with *this* relationship and *that* relationship. Instead, you will experience real vitality, not for a moment, but for a lifetime. We do this by reclaiming and integrating life's primal source of vitality—our sexual energy. This is what it means to *live in orgasm*.

When you live in orgasm, you live with a sense of what psychologists call *agency*, where you are the determiner of your own destiny. You have choice. You are an active agent, cocreating the world around you in flow. You release the need for stability, for control and predictability. As waves emerge, you ride them, innately understanding where the energy *wants to go* and flowing along with it. Though the ground beneath you shifts, it doesn't matter because you are able to shift with it.

It is from this space that we are able to truly welcome all that comes. To drop our judgment and resistance. Nothing is unwelcome, undesirable, or inconvenient. All is simply alive. We no longer need to tread carefully. Gone is the desire to be invisible, the need to be liked or to appear helpless. We no longer seek to constrict life, trying to control what's supposed to be. Instead, we can let all things be as they are. We can live in truth, dropping our masks and showing ourselves to the world honestly, without pretense. And though, in the immediate, others may be taken off guard by our own lack of guardedness, this is the seed and the source of trust—when we show others our true self. We begin to trust life, and it trusts us in turn.

When we open to sexual energy, when we claim and integrate it into our being, we access our purpose, our drive, our leadership, our own power. This energy is our wellspring, and it fuels us completely.

This is total freedom. Orgasm offers a direct path there. But how do we cultivate this power living in our own body? In the next section, we will dive into the practice of Orgasmic Meditation, the fastest, most reliable, repeatable, and safest method to access flow and the mystical state, a profound sense of understanding and satisfaction at the core of our power. This has been the experience of myself and thousands of OM practitioners and has also been shown through rigorous scientific analysis (which we'll explore in detail in the next chapter).

The Practice of Orgasmic Meditation (OM)

OM, pronounced "ohm," is a structured, attention-training practice conducted between two people who are following a predefined set of detailed instructions. The practice involves one person, the "stroker," gently stroking the clitoris of the "strokee" for 15 minutes while both place their attention on the point of contact and notice what they feel.

The clitoris is estimated to have 10,000 nerve endings, the highest concentration of nerve endings in the entire human anatomy,[3] making it a powerful physical tether to our attention. As we increase our capacity to maintain attention on this most highly sensational part of the body, our energy organizes in such a way that we can meet life more skillfully, understanding what

3. Franny White, "Pleasure-Producing Human Clitoris Has More Than 10,000 Nerve Fibers: First Known Count of Human Clitoral Nerve Fibers Could Improve Health, Sexual Function," *Oregon Health & Science University*, October 27, 2022, https://news.ohsu.edu/2022/10/27/pleasure-producing-human-clitoris-has-more -than-10-000-nerve-fibers.

is needed in each moment, and how to apply it. We become fully present and adept at existing in the here and now, at relating to life as it is actually happening. Not trying to change it or mold it to how we want it to be, but to meet it as it is. As author and meditator Wendy Palmer wrote of attention, "Energy tends to go where there is the most excitement, most clarity, most intensity. . . . By focusing our attention, we can stabilize ourselves." Willa Blythe Baker put it poetically: "The here and now is the very stuff of liberation."

Orgasmic Meditation (OM) is a structured, partnered meditation practice designed to cultivate attention, connection, and optimal arousal, and release the flow of erotic energy so that we can live in the ongoing orgasmic state. OM follows a precise sequence: One person, the stroker, gently strokes the clitoris of the other person, the strokee, for 15 minutes, while both place their attention on the point of contact and notice what they feel. The practice takes place in a "nest"—a setup with a blanket, pillows, and a zafu (meditation cushion), and has clear protocols ensuring a repeatable container.

Like meditation, yoga, and breathwork, OM trains the nervous system to register subtle and nuanced information and expand attention. However, the simple yet powerful form of engagement in OM harnesses the immense neural and energetic potential of the clitoris, training the mind to stay present in heightened sensation.

OM is the fastest, most reliable, repeatable, and safest method to access flow and the mystical state—a profound sense of understanding and satisfaction at the core of our power. While deep states of presence have traditionally been achieved through slow and disciplined methods like meditation or yoga, or through high-risk methods like extreme sports and psychedelics, OM offers a direct and sustainable pathway.

Rather than focusing on climax, OM expands one's ability to stay in the heightened, ongoing state of orgasm—where sensation and awareness deepen to bring us into closer connection with others and the world. The practice builds the capacity for resilience and flow, so that these qualities can be integrated beyond the OM session leading to more engagement with all aspects of everyday life.

Through regular practice, OM enhances the body's ability to process and channel energy. By harnessing the body's most primal impulse—erotic energy—OM bootstraps biology to create a direct pathway to one's own power. This practice cultivates an inner steadiness that affords a great courage, such that individuals do not abandon themselves or others—even in moments of difficulty. Rather than retreating, they welcome a life of deeper intimacy and enhanced emotional regulation.

The OM takes place in a nest, consisting of an arrangement of a blanket, pillows, and a zafu (meditation cushion). The practice involves the strokee removing her lower garments and lying down in the nest while the stroker, either a man or woman, remains fully clothed and sits beside her. The stroker follows a prescribed set of instructions and strokes the strokee's clitoris with the tip of their left index finger for 15 minutes. The stroker wears disposable latex or nitrile gloves and places a dab of lube on their left index finger and right thumb, which is placed at the strokee's introitus, where it rests for the OM. The stroke with the index finger is simple, brushing up and down against the clitoris, not any more firmly than the pressure you would use to stroke your eyelid. The tip of the finger remains in contact with the clitoris for the duration of the OM. For the final two minutes, the stroker will stroke with their emphasis downward, using firmer pressure and slightly longer strokes to transition to the end of the OM. After 15 minutes, the stroker applies grounding pressure with their palm and then uses a small towel to remove excess lube.

In OM, the roles of **strokee** and **stroker** are distinct yet equally essential, each carrying specific responsibilities and qualities of attention.

- The Strokee is the person whose clitoris is being stroked during the practice of OM. They focus their awareness on the point of contact between their clitoris and the stroker's finger. The strokee's role is not passive but rather an active engagement with their own body and the sensations that arise.

- The Stroker is the person stroking the strokee's clitoris during the practice of OM. Their role is one of precise attention and responsiveness. The stroker applies a deliberate, controlled stroke with their index finger, maintaining steady contact for 15 minutes. Their task is not to "make something happen" but to tune in to the strokee, adjusting as needed.

Together, the strokee and stroker create a dynamic feedback loop of sensation, awareness, communication (done in a specific way), and connection. Attention itself becomes the bridge to deeper states of consciousness and flow.

For most meditation practitioners, the focus is on the breath. Over time, that can have its effects. But the breath is a weak signal—the sensation is relatively low. The focused, intentional stroking of the clitoris is a very strong signal. During the OM, the strokee may often ask for a lighter stroke or firmer, faster or slower, a little to the left or right, more energetically "up" or "down" to adjust the stroke in just such a way that the sensation of finger to clitoris exactly matches the quality of energy in the body and the state of mind, directing its attention to the stroke at optimal arousal—enough that our awareness comes alive in vibrant detail, but not so high that we contract against it. We call it being "on the spot." The tactile sensation meets the energy of our body and mind in a way that we are able to totally relax while in a heightened state of arousal and vivid awareness.

When we are on the spot, we feel everything. As the stroke comes fully into the spot, it may feel like everything suddenly drops away and becomes quiet. All mental chatter and physical discomfort vanishes. There is no more motion. We feel an electromagnetic hum that begins in the clitoris and moves throughout the whole body. The stroker's finger becomes an exquisite sensor, and our clitoris exquisitely sensed.

When we get on the spot, there is a dynamic quality to the impact we have on each other. We find ourselves connected to the whole of the universe and the whole of the universe flowing through us. Each person impacts the other with subtle openings and closings. This is what OM trains us for, the world of connection where the possibility exists for a feedback loop of connection and sensation. In OM, we can experience and acknowledge directly that we profoundly affect each other, that we can move and be moved with gentleness, and that we can build something together.

As the strokee, we lean our attention in and allow the connection to move through us. When the stroker moves with our spot, there is an interior feeling like swaying in unison with music. We progressively feel more liquid, as though the finger is moving through a pool; what started as a distinct physical sensation, pressure, or heat now occurs as waves.

When the tactile sense begins to wane or the brightness of our awareness begins to dim, we can request to change a variable again, sometimes intuitively, sometimes through trial and error, until we find the next resonant stroke. During a single OM, it's typical for these peaks and changes to the stroke to occur more times than you can keep track of to stay in tune with the dynamism of the spot.

The last few minutes of the OM are spent stroking with the conscious intention to come back down, using slower, heavier, "down" strokes. At the end of the 15 minutes, the stroker lifts their finger from the clitoris and then applies "grounding pressure," placing the palm of their hand over the strokee's genitals and up toward the strokee's head for a few seconds. The pressure relieves the genitals of engorgement and helps smooth out the more energizing stroking portion of the OM. The OM partners then sit up and each share a "frame," a brief description of a sensation from during the OM, creating a feedback loop between partners and developing a bridge back into the orgasmic experience. We are training to live from orgasm; the bridge we build is the bridge home.

Orgasmic Meditation is like a steroid for attention training, allowing you to build this muscle much faster. It is visceral rather than conceptual, interacting directly with your nervous system. We don't *contemplate* enlightenment and expansion, we *become* it. When we allow the energy of the sensation to permeate our consciousness, when we allow that signal to guide us home, we come into deep and lasting connection with the energy of life. That is the power we learn to embody and direct.

Regular practitioners choose OM because, as previously mentioned, it's the fastest, most reliable, repeatable, and safest method for access to flow and the mystical state. In fact, most people who practice regularly don't OM just for the sensation of stroking a clitoris or having their clitoris stroked. If these results could be replicated by stroking an elbow or talking our way there, the practice would be designed around that. While the *idea* of OM might seem scandalous or lascivious, that's a far cry from the actual, embodied experience of bringing our full and conscious awareness to the presence of sensation. By harnessing the sexual impulse through this highly protocoled practice, individuals are able to safely and sustainably do what previously was attained slowly, through modalities such as meditation or yoga, or involving high-risk activities like extreme sports or psychedelics. Through the practice of OM, we build the muscle memory to live in the mystical and flow states continuously, ultimately leading to a life of flourishing.

The effect of OM is a total metamorphosis of the way we think, feel, and apprehend. In the orgasmic state, you align with things as they actually are rather than your concept of them or any desires and perceptions about how they should be.

At the cancer care facility where I work, my boss encourages everyone—both staff and patients—to meditate. There, they talk about "not being in your mind" for two minutes, and encourage that practice five times a day. And so we pause, and we tell ourselves, "Don't think . . .

Don't think . . ." And what happens? You know the drill—you can't get out of your head! You can't escape your thoughts. So they encourage us to put our focus on our breathing, or to put our focus on our hearts. But I uncovered a much more effective approach . . . I put my attention on my genitals.

For one, that's a lot more fun than focusing on your breath. But as a longtime OM practitioner, I understand how enlivening it is to open myself to what's there and let the energy of that space in my body open.

I had a patient who had breast cancer. Her daughter would come visit her and she was extremely resistant to the idea of alternative medicine. She wanted her mother to try chemo and radiation—the traditional Western approaches. But the mother didn't want to. Still, her daughter came to support her. During one visit, it actually came up in conversation that all of this focus on the breath was, well, boring. So I told them, "Well, I focus on the genitals instead. I focus on sex. That's a lot more fun, right?" The daughter paused for a minute and then nodded. "Yeah," she said, "I really like that." And the next thing you know, she was opening to the idea of other approaches.

It can be a bit disarming at first, because we're not supposed to talk about sex. But sex is *life*. And what are we trying to do in this care facility—we're trying to help people heal so they can go on living, ideally more richly and openly than before. Because being closed off and shut down is part of what got them to us in the first place. The opening is part of healing.

To be clear, OM *isn't* sex. It's not meant to be a substitute for sex; it's not foreplay to sex. Orgasmic Meditation is exactly that—a meditation practice where we cultivate our orgasm. And again, when we say "orgasm" we mean the *whole* of our orgasm; all the expressions of sexual energy within our alive, erotic being. This is our creativity, our genius. It is the same power that flows through an artist when she finds herself in tune with her canvas, or the musician at her violin. The flow and creativity of a waitress during the Friday night dinner rush, doing five things at once while carrying more than you'd even imagine she could, and doing it all with grace and a knowing smile. But here, in the practice, all the extra is set aside and we connect with the essence of the creative spark that resides within us by the most direct path we have available to it.

OM is a goalless practice, meaning there is no particular outcome you are trying to achieve. Unlike most sex or masturbation, in OM, climax is not the end goal. OM is about developing focused attention and cultivating our sexual energies so that we can awaken into the orgasmic state. Where all the barriers, the repression, the judgment, the expectation, and all forms of unprocessed energy are released so that you can be in perpetual flow with and enlivened by the energy of life. It is from this space you will taste true freedom and realize no one is holding you back. When we can maintain our focus and our receptivity in states of high arousal, where our nervous system is fully online and engaged, we feel a readiness to meet whatever comes. We know our consciousness is strong enough, supple enough, responsive enough, and open enough to handle the situation. And when we can be this receptive to life, and to others, we know that no other person can ever have control over us. No matter what you experience, you will remain yourself—fully present, and fully alive.

Attention is the skill of directing awareness with precision and presence. While meditation, breathwork, yoga, and other mindfulness practices develop attention, Orgasmic Meditation refines it in a unique way—training the mind to remain fully engaged with sensation rather than chasing or avoiding it. OM develops active, volitional attention.

In OM, attention functions as both an anchor and a conduit. The stroker and strokee place their attention on the point of contact, attuning to the subtlest shifts in sensation. This deep noticing amplifies awareness, creating a feedback loop of energy between partners. As attention strengthens, it enables the practitioner to track and release stored tension, dissolving tumescence and allowing energy to flow freely.

Mastery of attention in OM progresses through stages: first, curious attention, where the practitioner becomes aware of sensation; then, flow attention, where they synchronize effortlessly with the body's natural rhythms; and finally, liberated attention, where stored energy is fully transformed—turning suppressed desire into creative power.

Ultimately, attention in OM is not just about noticing—it is about engaging with sensation as a tool for transformation. It helps practitioners remain present even during moments of discomfort, allowing them to meet intensity with openness rather than reactivity. This ability is a foundation of personal power, extending beyond OM and reshaping how practitioners engage with life itself, fostering deeper connection, clarity, and freedom.

OM has the power to align us with what moves us most deeply, within ourselves and in the world. OM is the answer to our epidemic of loneliness and disconnection, creating a mindful, empathic feedback loop between two people. It is the means through which we can transmute the toxicity of the world around us to experience life differently. It is the means through which we can literally rewire ourselves, reorganizing our nervous system so that we can be more open to connection. So we can experience ourselves more richly, and share that abundance with others. The fact we hold back in seeking to connect with our deeper self means we also hold back from each other. It's similar to how science has shown that when you numb one feeling, you necessarily numb them all.[4] And when we isolate ourselves from one another, we isolate ourselves from life. The practice of OM shows us what it means to belong to one another, to life, and to Love.

As you are no doubt sensing, to welcome freedom is not a small thing. It is a journey—one that can often feel perilous because of the vulnerability inherent to it. But once you taste that freedom, the limitations you left behind feel like a small sacrifice.

As Helen Schucman put it, "Our task is not to seek for love, but merely to find all the barriers within yourself that you have built against it."[5] The practice of OM will help you identify and dissolve these barriers. It will liberate you from your limited sense of self and deliver you into the arms of your power. From that space, you will become all that you are capable of being.

4. Geoffrey R. O. Durso, Andrew Luttrell, and Baldwin M. Way, "Over-the-Counter Relief from Pains and Pleasures Alike: Acetaminophen Blunts Evaluation Sensitivity to Both Negative and Positive Stimuli," *Psychological Science 26*, no. 6 (2015): 750–758, accessed [March 27, 2025], https://pmc.ncbi.nlm.nih.gov/articles/PMC4515109/.
5. Helen Schucman, *A Course in Miracles* (Foundation for Inner Peace, 1976), T-16.IV.6:1.

You will experience the life that you long for, and that has been longing for you.

> We will be discussing OM more throughout this book, but it is not meant to serve as step-by-step training. If you would like to learn how to OM, the Institute of OM offers the OM App on the Apple Store or online at https://om.instituteofom.com. For more in-depth training in Orgasmic Meditation and its related philosophy and programs, visit the Eros Platform at https://erosplatform.com.

CHAPTER 2

OM Under the Microscope

Sure, sex *feels good*—at least sometimes, for some of us—but there's an inherent sense that there is something deeper there. More specifically, what if a technique based in sexuality could improve parts of our lives that we may not necessarily associate with sex? That's the question that's attracted some of the world's leading neuroscientists to study OM. Can the promise of real, lasting healing live up to the hype?

Since Masters and Johnson's groundbreaking work on the human sexual response in the 1950s and '60s, science has largely been quiet on the subject of human sexuality, particularly studies on partnered sexual response. As UCLA neuroscientist Dr. Nicole Prause observes, "Sex research in the U.S. is no joke. The United States is extremely hostile to this type of research."[6]

But for a few courageous scientists, the prospect of a safe, replicable technique that can reliably unlock human healing has fortunately proved too powerful to ignore. As neuroscientist Dr. Andrew Newberg writes in his book, *Sex, God, and the Brain: How Sexual Pleasure Gave Birth to Religion and a Whole Lot*

---

6. "The Science of Orgasmic Meditation: A Path to Deeper Connection and Joy," virtual lecture, posted December 21, 2023, by IOM Foundation, YouTube, 44:42, https://www.youtube.com/watch?v=mLnktDzkYk8.

More, he has long been convinced that a tangible, biological intersection exists between spirituality and sexuality. Yet an exact physiological pathway or link proved elusive.

He needed data, and to get it, he would have to find a practice that invokes both—that actually *uses* our sexuality to connect us to a spiritual state. An obvious choice would be Tantric yoga, but there were multiple challenges. For one, you can't put two people who are engaging in sex in an MRI machine. Also, the practice needed to be more specifically defined, boundaried, and time-limited. It would require a safe container, so the person engaging in it could truly experience it. It's tough to impossible to have a transcendent experience in a science lab (or so he thought). Plus, there would have to be an ability to actually integrate any healing that was experienced. Spiritual epiphanies and breakthroughs are wonderful, but if they don't result in lasting change, they amount to only a brief respite from our suffering, as users of recreational drugs have long known.

Enter OM.

When I reached out to Dr. Newberg to see if he'd be interested in studying it, I'd already had the door slammed in my face multiple times. As Dr. Prause had observed, anything even remotely to do with sex is met with skepticism from most scientists. Even if they *wanted* to study it, no traditional organization would grant funding for it. Dr. Newberg was different. As he writes in his book *Sex, God, and the Brain: How Sexual Pleasure Gave Birth to Religion and a Whole Lot More*, his initial reaction to my call was skeptical.

> "My first thought was, 'That sounds a little weird.' But in my years of researching spiritual practices and experiences, I had gotten pretty used to things that were weird. In fact, I have often thought that the phrase, 'that seems weird,' may

be one of the most important statements leading to big scientific discoveries, so I was also intrigued. As I reflected on how she was describing this unique practice that combined sexual stimulation and meditation, I thought to myself, 'Could this be the practice that combines sexuality and spirituality that I have been hoping to study for the past 30 years? Could this provide invaluable data helping us understand the link between sexuality and spirituality?'"

As it turned out, OM proved to be precisely the platform he'd been looking for to examine the biological and neurological mechanisms through which sexuality and transcendent experiences are connected in humans. Not just connected, in fact. As research has now revealed, sexuality may be the very mechanism through which we are biologically equipped to access what is best in us—our fullest potential.

It's Not Sex, It's Better

The beauty of OM, as researchers and practitioners alike have realized, is that while it engages sexuality, it is not sex. Therefore, it is unencumbered by a lot of the baggage and self-criticisms we may feel toward ourselves in relation to sex, as well as the expectations and communication issues that we associate with sex. Instead, by reducing the practice to the bare essentials, OM harnesses the pure sexual impulse and directs it with laser focus.

In fact, that's exactly what OM is—a practice of focus and connection, of attention and openness. Put more clinically, it is a structured attention-training practice that develops our capacity to attune to all of life equally and simultaneously, allowing us to experience intimacy with each moment.

How often does life feel like too much to you? How frequently do you feel overwhelmed, as if you don't have enough bandwidth to handle what's happening, or to process what has occurred in the past? OM opens your aperture. Arousal, when experienced in a container where we feel safe, allows us to broaden our lens so that we can allow life to exist in its wholeness—so that *you* can be in wholeness, no longer having to hold back or suppress the energy that wants to move through you.

This is the magical combination of elements that OM brings together. The regular, set structure and protocols of the OM "container" create a feeling of safety and predictability that allows the participants to relax. The practice is pared down to its absolute essentials, which discourages distractions that might take focus away from the point of connection between clitoris and tip of the finger. And finally, the element of arousal that rises from the sensation is able to be experienced purely, without the "meaning" and "justification" and "context" we usually assign to it.

> Orgasmic Meditation takes place within a structured, standardized set of agreements known as the ***container***. Much like the rules of a game—where soccer forbids the use of hands or chess dictates specific movements—the OM container defines the practice's boundaries. Without these fundamental parameters, OM would no longer be OM.
>
> The container's primary function is to relax vigilance—the constant scanning for potential danger. By establishing predictability and safety, the container signals to the nervous system that external threats have already been mitigated. Over time, repeated OM sessions within the container allow vigilance to

gradually relax, giving practitioners greater access to sensation, connection, and self-awareness.

Each aspect of the container is nonnegotiable, providing a stable structure that allows practitioners to fully immerse in the experience. Key elements include:

- A 15-minute timed stroking period.
- The stroker remains fully clothed, while the strokee removes only the necessary clothing to expose the genitals.
- The stroker must wear gloves, regardless of their relationship with the strokee.
- The steps of OM must be followed in order, without omission.

By ensuring consistency, the container eliminates ambiguity, prevents distractions, and maintains the integrity of the practice. Rather than restricting freedom, the container creates a reliable framework that enables deeper presence, allowing practitioners to move beyond habitual defenses and access new levels of intimacy and transformation.

*For a full list of all parts of the container, please see "The Container and Form of Orgasmic Meditation," which can be found in Nicole Daedone's *The Eros Sutras, Volume 3: Orgasmic Meditation,* as well as online at https://erosplatform.com/volumes/volume-3/sutras/the-container.

What we discover in the raw experience of arousal is very different from the story we often assign to our feelings, and particularly our strong feelings. Arousal creates a kind of heat and acts like a rising tide, lifting all boats—with arousal, amusement can become ecstatic joy; depression may transform to a poignant wail or even rage. And while we tend to think of our emotions along a simple line from good to bad, at these high states of arousal, these emotions organize to take on their own meaning and we aren't able to judge them along the same yardstick as our emotions in low states of arousal. The intensity of sensation reveals the underlying architecture of our emotions, revealing the continuity and overlap between such disparate sentiments as joy and sadness, disgust and desire.

Arousal gives us the power to transcend and integrate beyond the boundaries of what we permit ourselves to experience in our day-to-day lives. There is a perceived safety to remaining within the confines of known experience, but we can also recognize the simple wisdom Anaïs Nin once expressed: "And the day came when the risk to remain tight in a bud was more painful than the risk it took to blossom."

When we unplug from experience, the result is a life that feels gray and, well, lifeless. Our everyday approaches to resolving this state of mind and reanimating our lives leaves much to be desired. Most of our ways of addressing depression, anxiety, burnout, trauma, and whatever else ails us mentally and emotionally steer us away from arousal. For starters, our society places a primacy on the brain and logical thought. We have sidelined both spirituality and sexuality in favor of endless analysis. But we have issues we simply cannot think our way out of. OM gives us access to what lives inside us, but that only "comes out at night." That shies away from attempts to intellectualize it. To quote poet Mary Oliver, OM speaks to "the soft animal of our body."

Then, there is the matter of psychiatric medications. Too often, pharmaceuticals attempt to resolve our dis-ease by muting it. But by turning down the volume on some emotions, you mute all of them. Our entire capacity to feel is silenced. Perhaps we don't feel quite so bad, but we don't feel good, either. OM, on the other hand, expands our access to positive emotional states. It broadens our capacity for happiness while decreasing our feelings of negativity.

It does this by using our sexual response to access different mental states. Through OM, we can experience flow. We can access spiritual experiences including a sense of oneness. We can feel connection and safety. And we can heal.

I experienced a lot growing up in the ghettos of the Bronx. In addition to the abuse I endured, I witnessed a lot of violence and drug use. Life at home was chaotic. My mother was suicidal. She'd been battered. Had ten kids by the time she was thirty. The adults in my life were completely out of control. That meant I felt like I needed to take control. As a kid, I went up into my head to escape the chaos I felt in my body and in my experience.

At age nineteen, I got on a Greyhound bus and got as far away as possible, to LA. Fortunately, by roundabout means which I later realized were simply the flow of life looking out for my best interests, in California I ended up working with a skilled therapist. She not only helped me start to unpack all the trauma I'd experienced personally, along with all of the oppression and racism due to my mixed Puerto Rican, Cuban, and Dominican heritage, she also helped me organize my life so I could finish college.

At some point, I had this ah-ha! moment where suddenly I knew I was capable of much more than the people around me had told me. Eventually, I set my sights on medical school. Medical school! I didn't get there until I was thirty-five, but really, there's no such thing as too late. I had a six-month-old at the time, and my husband had just died. There's also no such thing as perfect timing. I was there, so to me that meant the timing was perfect.

In my life, I pushed down a lot of my experiences. I pushed down and pushed on. But I was always connected to my impulses, and I followed them. I didn't think too much about whether something made sense or not—if it drove me or captured my attention, I pursued it.

After I became licensed, I joined the staff of a hospital in Oakland. Eight years in, I had to stand (literally) for an oral exam in order to become fully licensed in surgery. Only, I failed. So I tried again. And I failed again. I knew the material, but I would just get up in front of these men who were supposed to be judging my intelligence and my ability, and I would just go blank. Finally, I realized the problem. In medical education, like in so much of life, they teach you to memorize everything in your head, then repeat it when you're called to. But I don't think with my head. I don't learn with my head. I learn with my body. I feel the information, and I assimilate it. When I had to stand before these people whose job it was to judge my ability to think, I shut down. I couldn't access my real wisdom.

To access all of our knowledge and all our capabilities requires access to our body. And access to our body requires that we feel safe. And very few of us ever know what it is to truly feel safe. OM helps us experience safety, perhaps for the first time. That becomes something we carry inside ourselves. A space we can return to.

For women, especially, we know something is true because we can feel truth in our bodies. But if we're cut off from our bodies, we're cut off from this way of knowing and of relating to the world. That's one of the reasons I left mainstream medicine—there's little space for actual truth. We don't heal through what's in textbooks. Yes, they can help us understand some of the specific mechanisms that are at work in our bodies. But we *heal* through connection—with ourselves and others.

As Dr. Newberg explains, elements of human physiology have long been utilized to fuel meditative states. Breathing, walking, visualizing, guided imagery . . . Sexual energy is simply another, more powerful means of purposefully engaging elements of our inherent design. It may be, he speculates, that sexuality and spirituality share the same neurobiological basis in the brain. This may explain why so many religions get hung up on sex—because they utilize the same bandwidth. But rather than seeing sex and spirituality as competitors, characterizing them as *partners* would enable us to access the ultimate benefits of both in terms of human flourishing.

Before we discuss these benefits in detail—as revealed by scientific study—let's get specific about the practice. What, exactly, makes OM special?

The Mechanics of OM

To those unfamiliar with the practice, the very name *Orgasmic Meditation* conjures up the idea of sex. But similar to how we can distinguish climax as a particular *aspect* of the entirety of orgasm, we can distinguish between the arousal of sexual energy in our body from the act of sex itself. We are engaging directly with the energy that has us feel *turned on*—whether that's sexually or switched on in life, work, fun.

In the same way that there is a "container" that describes the three-dimensional aspects of OM, there is instruction for how the OM partners focus their attention and engage in the practice that is the most efficient way to experience OM's benefits. You can think of OM as the mechanism through which we access the *state of being* that is orgasm.

Simply put, OM is a structured attention-training practice following a specific set of instructions. The practice involves one person, the stroker, gently stroking the clitoris of the other person, the strokee, for 15 minutes while both place their attention on the point of contact and notice what they feel. The stroker must have a finger and the strokee must have a clitoris.

OM is not intended to be heterocentric; it is simply that the practice works in conjunction with our basic biological and neurological wiring. Therefore, it's required that the strokee have a clitoris. The sexual orientation and gender identity of the participants does not matter, and participants may be in a partnered relationship or not.

The goal of OM is not to achieve climax, and strokees may or may not experience climax during an OM session. To be clear, the stroker is not working to have the strokee "get off." In many ways, climax is beside the point, which is one of the reasons the practice is not encumbered by performance anxiety or the expectations that so often burden our sexual encounters.

Instead, the aim is to develop heightened awareness through expanded sensitivity and capacity of attention to the physical sensations experienced as both partners place their awareness on the stroke and pay attention to what they feel in their own body. It is this deep noticing from both the stroker and strokee that connects their energy, the energy of attention.

The stroker is using the tip of their index finger to lightly stroke the strokee's clitoris for exactly 15 minutes. The practice takes place in a *nest*, which is a basic setup of blankets and pillows arranged in such a way that both participants are comfortable.

During the session, the strokee "simply" notices and stays present with the sensations. I put that in quotes because, as an OM practitioner—really, any meditation practitioner—can tell you, maintaining your awareness on a single point of focus for 15 minutes can be difficult, to say the least. With a signal as strong and clear as contact with your clitoris, it can be even more challenging to stay with the sensation. Often, we want to get lost in wanting something—something different, or something more. If you've ever done classic meditation, you know that clinging is a major obstacle. It's even more powerful in OM, but that provides an opportunity. When you're able to meet this desire to grip and grasp in its raw, untamed form, over time you're able to uproot it fully, rather than simply defuse it in the moment.

That's one of the reasons OM is so incredibly effective; it helps us build the muscle of presence, and our ability to stay connected, whatever arises, *while in various states of arousal*. And so we can take that capability with us out of the OM nest and into the world. We begin to see and live life in full technicolor, open to every experience and sensation. Stressors and challenges still exist, but we no longer have to suppress or block them. When we meet what at first feels like an obstacle, we learn to recognize it as the way—the very path itself—and we move forward into it. We no longer resist life, we partner with it. As this familiarity and camaraderie with life energy expands, we learn to direct these forces thoughtfully, powerfully, and with purpose.

I found OM in 2012, when I was 53 years old. When I did, I saw that God was aligning everything all along. OM gave me a context for understanding and purposefully directing the energy I had always felt; the energy was always there, guiding me. I feel like my life is a miracle. Even the things that were traumatic eventually brought me gifts. All this time, the wisdom of my body was at work. Even when I was trying to live in my mind, it was always helping me. At any moment, the same thing is happening in everyone's life. OM helps us to understand the forces that are active in our lives—to speak life's language.

But how can a basic 15-minute practice impact us in such dramatic ways? Brain imaging is beginning to answer that question.

The Ego Falls Away

There is an ancient Mesopotamian myth, possibly older than written language itself. It is the myth of Inanna, the goddess of love, war, and fertility, Queen of Heaven and Earth. In the story, Inanna descends into the underworld to visit her sister, Ereshkigal, Queen of the Dead. To pass through each of the bolted gates, Inanna must remove a piece of her royal finery—a crown, a necklace, a breastplate—each symbolizing a layer of her identity. Stripped of every outer aspect of herself, Inanna becomes confused and helpless until she surrenders to the immutable laws of life and death, a power greater than anything she had held onto in her journey to her sister.

As Jung points out, Inanna's sister Ereshkigal is not truly separate from Inanna but another aspect of her being—the shadow her above-world being is inextricably linked to. This is a truth Inanna can only experience once she has shed her outward contrivances. When Inanna finally ascends from the underworld, she is both humbled and empowered, having integrated every aspect of herself, including the feminine energy of life and death. She emerges as Queen of Heaven, Earth, and the Dead, her suffering transmuted into transformation.

This allegory demonstrates the spiritual path told in countless spiritual and religious stories, of releasing the self we are convinced is *us* only to find something more fulfilling comes alive in its absence. It was a path that might seem in contradiction to scientific inquiry but is exactly what Dr. Andrew Newberg and his field of *neurotheology* have come to study. And thanks to the latest breakthroughs in neuroscience research, he and his fellow researchers are creating a new cartography for spiritual experience.

As Dr. Andrew Newberg notes in his book, *Sex, God, and the Brain*, the brain typically lights up during sex, showing more activity in multiple areas. Conversely, with meditation, the brain largely quiets down. As studies looking at what goes on in the brains of OM practitioners have now revealed, activity during OM more closely mirrors meditation than sex. He writes:

> "When we looked at the entire group, we found several important and significant changes that occurred during the OM practice. We saw decreases in frontal lobe activity, as well as decreases in parietal lobe activity. These

changes are important because . . . such decreases more resemble a meditative practice rather than sexual stimulation. In fact, studies of sexual stimulation typically demonstrate a brain becoming more and more active. But during OM, the brain seems to start quieting down in most areas.

"The decrease in frontal lobe activity is probably associated with a sense of letting go or release. As we have described earlier, the frontal lobes are involved in helping us focus attention on whatever tasks we have at hand. Studies of meditation and prayer that involve intense focus on various objects or phrases typically result in increased frontal lobe activity. However, practices involving a sense of release or letting go have been associated with decreased frontal lobe activity. Interestingly, decreased frontal lobe activity has also been reported in flow states as well as in highly creative states such as jazz improvisation. These are all states in which a person feels as if their own consciousness is no longer in control of the process, and it is simply happening to them. They are along for the ride."[7]

As one practitioner reported, for her, one of the major benefits of OM has been this ability to *let go*. Elsewhere in life, she'd often felt the need to seek out increasingly intense situations and experiences to essentially force herself to feel. This is a common approach among those of us attempting to break through the numbness we experience when our energy is blocked or restricted. In OM, she said, people felt a sense of release or letting go. Instead of going out and forcing experience, she could be still and receive it, both figuratively and literally.

7. Andrew Newberg, M.D., *Sex, God, and the Brain,* (Turner Publishing, 2024), chap. 5, Kindle.

The basic act of being fully present is surprisingly power-ful. In a study headed by geneticist Dr. Vivian Siegel at MIT, both strokers and strokees described peak spiritual experiences similar to those described by people who had taken a dose of the hallucinogen psilocybin, which is being investigated as a treatment for mental health disorders. The study used the thirty-question Mystical Experience Questionnaire ("MEQ") developed by Roland Griffiths, PhD., a professor in the Departments of Psychiatry and Neurosciences at the Johns Hopkins University School of Medicine. Griffiths originally designed the MEQ to quantify the subject experience of psychedelics and spiritual practices and used it in a string of groundbreaking experiments around psilocybin.

The MEQ is designed to quantify four aspects of mystical experience: mysticism (feeling of "oneness"), positive mood, transcendence of time and space, and ineffability, or the sense that an experience cannot be described adequately in words. High MEQ scores have correlated with promising treatments for a number of medical conditions. For example, prior studies using the MEQ have shown that psychedelics trigger a mystical-type experience, and the strength of the mystical experience has correlated with potential treatments for nicotine addiction, depression, and other mood and drug-use disorders.

This particular study consisted of two different surveys. In the first, 780 participants were asked to bring to mind "a single powerful OM" experience, then complete the questionnaire. On average, participants in this survey reported having moderate to strong mystical experiences. To some extent, the intensity of their experiences correlated with how frequently they engaged in OM. Of the participants in this study, *62 percent reported having a complete mystical experience during an OM.*

For the second survey, fifty-six couples completed the questionnaire immediately following an OM. Participants in this survey also reported moderate mystical experiences, with no statistically significant difference in total mysticism scores between strokers and strokees.

Scientists also studied this phenomenon from another angle, analyzing approximately 1,500 journal entries written by various OM practitioners describing their experiences in the practice. Through statistical analysis and data visualization techniques, the researchers found consistent themes that mirrored the core characteristics of mystical experience. Throughout the writing, OMers documented experiences of a sense of union with all things and altered perceptions of time and sensation, a sense of sacredness or ecstasy and bliss, or the sense of being guided by an external force. The findings suggest that Orgasmic Meditation is capable of inducing a mystical state that shares many traits with those produced by pharmacologically assisted methods.[8]

Dr. Siegel stated, "Given that OM apparently can trigger a mystical experience of similar power to psilocybin, and that psilocybin has shown promise in the treatment of mood and substance disorders, this study raises intriguing questions about whether OM might also be effective in the treatment of these disorders."[9]

---

8. Dr. Caroline Griggs and Rachel Pelletier, "Orgasmic Meditation and The Mystical Experience: A Case Study," preprint, SSRN, 2024, accessed February 28, 2025, https://ssrn.com/abstract=5120807.
9. Marisa Ward, "Study Finds Orgasmic Meditation Triggers Substantial 'Mystical Experience,' Which Has Been Linked to Treatment of Depression," BusinessWire, https://www.businesswire.com/news/home/20211130005924/en/Study-Finds-Orgasmic-Meditation-Triggers-Substantial-%E2%80%9CMystical-Experience%E2%80%9D-Which-Has-Been-Linked-to-Treatment-of-Depression.

OM liberates us from the mind that's keeping track and delivers us into a state of being and experiencing all that is true and present in the moment. We feel *in flow with life*.

In analyzing the brains of practitioners, Dr. Newberg also saw that another portion of the frontal lobes was affected during OM sessions—the anterior cingulate gyrus.[10] This area is believed to perform a mediating function between *executive processes* such as concentration and our emotions. Dr. Newberg explains that this, too, is similar to what the meditating brain looks like, and it indicates that OM may help us regulate our emotions.

Given these findings, it's not surprising that OM practitioners often report a decrease in depressive states and increase in positive mood. Flow states, themselves, are linked with greater levels of happiness and calm, a sense of clarity, greater emotional regulation, increased intrinsic motivation, and a feeling that perceived obstacles no longer exist.[11] When we feel depressed, we are looping a state of despair, where we believe that *this is how life is*. We experience extreme self-focus, unable to disconnect from our fragile ego. Flow states, such as those enabled by OM, clear these clouds, showing us that life has much more to offer us than agitation, anxiety, and rumination. We feel a sense of oneness that dwarfs our sense of self, and for a few glorious moments, our ego falls away. Yet though they are brief, these experiences change us, reorienting our outlook on life.

As a practitioner said, "A couple of months after I started a regular OM practice, my depression was gone. When I OM, my mind goes quiet and my body comes alive." It is that aliveness that reconnects us to life, and to hope, to the vibrant and the sensual that are all around us at every moment.

---

10. Newberg, *Sex, God, and the Brain*, 77.
11. "How to Achieve a Flow State," VeryWellMind, accessed January 26, 2025, https://www.verywellmind.com/what-is-flow-2794768.

Often, those plagued by anxiety and depression experience a double challenge. For one, there is *depressive rumination*—the endlessly looping negative thoughts that form a cage around our mind and heart. Then, there is *reward insensitivity*, where even when positive things happen, we're unable to fully absorb the joy that's present. All of the intensity we feel is negative, while we struggle to sustain positive emotions.

Many therapeutic methods seek to disconnect us from negative feeling states, but as I mentioned earlier, they don't simply unplug us from the bad, they throw the circuit breaker on all of our emotions, muting everything. The practice of OM helps us locate reality and increases our ability to feel and attend to it. We do not feel the need to try to change it; instead, we fully accept reality as it is, at every moment.

That doesn't mean every OM session *feels great* in the moment, or that the strokee is flooded only with sensations she would label as *good*. In reality, all kinds of feelings can arise in a given session. What OM does is train our ability to be with all of them. When we experience depression, we feel fragile, like life is too much. One of the ways OM helps to alleviate this feeling is by showing us that we can be present in all states, whether we're experiencing joy, curiosity, confusion, or challenge. It's similar to how, when we're driving a car and hit a patch of ice, we learn to turn *into* the skid. Instead of fighting it, we move closer, and in so doing, we learn a new kind of control. We regain our personal agency, and that doesn't require that everything in life *be* positive in order for us to *feel* positive about our lives.

In the practice of OM, we train a response that at first feels counterintuitive—not out of recklessness, but carefully and with consideration. There is no urgency. We simply go with the energy, moving into the heart or essence of the feeling. Thus, we learn to welcome life in all of its many forms. Everyday stressors no longer derail us. We no longer need to run from what feels uncomfortable. We no longer need to feel overwhelmed or numb. We learn we can meet each moment no matter what it holds and welcome it without judgment. From that space, we are free to use the life energy that's available to us to create something new. And because OM is a partnered practice, it also teaches us that we can create *together*.

The secure, grounded container for OM—a container built on total mutual consent and clear communication—allows for our full presence. It is this unique space that enables such a positive and profound experience. For many, the same is not true of sex.

The Good Parts of Sex

There is a wide divide between the experience OM aims to bring us to and the experiences most of us are used to in sex. To borrow a saying from writer and polymath John Perry Barlow, the difference between love and unconditional love is the difference between a very large number and infinity. That's the difference between sex—particularly as it's been designed and defined by masculine, phallocentric ideas of sex—and practicing pure orgasm.

Frequently, those who practice OM experience what they describe as a *coming back to life*. The body turns on and the blood rushes into your extremities after a deep cold. We feel enlivened as sensation returns. We are liberated. OM lets the blood rush back into our sexuality.

As Dr. Nicole Prause describes, sex research generally relies on pornography or fantasy to generate arousal, but there is a slew of emotions that accompany that arousal, including shame, anger, or other negative emotions. This can happen with sex as well, especially if we have a history of trauma, where our sexual circuitry may have been cross-linked to a variety of unwelcome thoughts, feelings, and sensations. But what Dr. Prause has discovered in her research that's unique to OM is its ability to give us access to the positive aspects of sexuality without the negative. "If you're someone who's had a trauma history, would this give you the ability to have an intense emotional experience?" Dr. Prause wondered, comparing the intense emotional, but strongly negative responses that cognitive processing therapy or exposure therapy often elicit for those patients. "If (OM) gives us another pathway to access some form of healing, maybe related to depression or post-traumatic stress disorders, that would be a huge win."[12]

This is an important distinction—the interventions we currently have available may change how much we feel, but they don't necessarily adjust whether we feel better or worse about an experience. Pills like antidepressants and anti-anxiety medications are designed to lessen those sensations, but in doing so, they can also mute *all* sensations, including arousal. Negative emotions may decrease, but so do positive emotions—an effect known as "emotional blunting."[13]

It shouldn't be surprising that SSRIs (selective serotonin reuptake inhibitors)—prescribed to treat depression, anxiety, and other mood disorders—affect arousal in ways that *usually* have an impact on the patient's sex life. NIH reports that more

12. Dr. Nicole Prause, "Positive vs Negative emotions in OM," virtual lecture, posted December 21, 2021, by Institute of OM, 02:34, https://vimeo.com/659259432/dd5aaff14b.
13. C. Langley, S. Armand, Q. Luo, et al., "Chronic escitalopram in healthy volunteers has specific effects on reinforcement sensitivity: a double-blind, placebo-controlled semi-randomised study," *Neuropsychopharmacology* 48 (2023): 664–670, https://doi.org/10.1038/s41386-022-01523-x.

than half of people who take SSRIs encounter problems with their sex lives,[14] and I would argue sex is a core component to our happiness! The idea that OM could decrease negative emotions while simultaneously increasing positive emotions is a "holy grail" of interventions, a custom pharmacy inside your own body without the negative side effects we can expect from pharmaceuticals.

To study OM, Dr. Nicole Prause partnered with Dr. Greg J. Siegle of the University of Pittsburgh. While Dr. Prause is a doctor of neuroscience and sexuality, Dr. Siegle is a professor of psychiatry and translational science, focusing on translating scientific discoveries into meaningful innovations for patients' mental conditions. Together, they studied OM through a broad lens, including cognitive tests before and after OMs, self-report surveys, and physiological measurements of participants during the OMs themselves, using tools like EEGs to measure brainwave activity and galvanic skin response to gauge arousal. After a year of research with 125 couples, they had accumulated broad and diverse research data that revealed surprising insights into the OM practice.

Some of the most powerful discoveries were realized months later by scientists who continued to analyze the data after the research phase had concluded. One such result was a correlation between adverse childhood experiences and the amount that OMing affected the practitioner. As Dr. Siegle and Dr. Prause write in their article published in the journal *Sexual and Relationship Therapy*, "Adverse childhood experiences (ACEs), such as child abuse, neglect, and family dysfunction,

---

14. Angel L. Montejo, Nieves Prieto, Rubén de Alarcón, *et al.* "Management Strategies for Antidepressant-Related Sexual Dysfunction: A Clinical Approach," *Journal of Clinical Medicine*, Oct 7;8(10):1640 (2019). https://pmc.ncbi.nlm.nih.gov/articles/PMC6832699.

are correlated with higher risk for a variety of poor physical and mental health outcomes, including decreased sexual satisfaction."[15] Some believe this is a follow-on from the anxiety and difficulty bonding that those who have experienced ACEs may demonstrate.

Analyzing their data, Dr. Prause and Dr. Siegle became curious about the alternative narrative they saw unfolding. Indeed, as their study demonstrated: "Following one session of OM, those who had experienced more ACEs, especially sexual molestation or assault, reported greater sexual arousal than those who had fewer ACEs. People with high ACEs were able to experience sexual pleasure in the environment evaluated."

This is an incredibly important finding for people who have experienced trauma in their early life and are worried about the impact it has on their adult sexual lives. Prause and Siegle's discovery bucks the narrative that trauma makes people "broken" and affirms the felt experience of men and women who might otherwise judge their body's arousal response as "bad" or "wrong."

So what is it that allows for OM participants who had experienced sexual trauma as a child to report *even higher levels* of arousal than subjects without any significant history of trauma? Prause and Siegle had a hypothesis. They noted that "apparent difficulties in sexual reactions associated with ACEs are attributable to contextual factors such as the risk and unpredictability inherent in many sexual encounter situations." After all, "Adverse childhood events lead to feelings that life, especially sexual experiences, are unpredictable and risky." But the clearly defined and agreed-upon container of OM offers a

---

15. Prause, N., H. Cohen, and G. J. Siegle. 2021. "Effects of Adverse Childhood Experiences on Partnered Sexual Arousal Appear Context Dependent." *Sexual and Relationship Therapy* 38 (3): 479–94, https://doi.org/10.1080/14681994.2021.1991907.

predictable structure and well-defined boundaries. Their findings show that "a structured sexual context is associated with increased sexual arousal in persons with . . . a trauma history."

As these results suggest, those who have suffered traumatic or adverse events in their past may choose to practice OM at least in part because it provides a safe, predictable space to enjoyably experience arousal. Among those who have experienced such trauma, it is common to have trouble either becoming aroused or staying with their arousal, as the rising tide of arousal can bring with it challenging feelings such as fear or anxiety. Yet as Dr. Prause and Dr. Siegle have shown, OM practitioners who previously experienced trauma had an expanded ability to stay with their arousal and take pleasure in it. Negative emotions were either less likely to appear or were less aversive. And to be able to experience this in connection with another person is, for many, nothing short of transformative.

OM and Healing Trauma

The groundbreaking research published by Dr. Nicole Prause and Dr. Greg Siegle caught the attention of many in the science community from a variety of disciplines. One of those was Dr. Daniel Kriegman, a psychologist who formerly served as chief psychologist and the director of supervision and training at the Massachusetts Treatment Center for Sexually Dangerous Offenders. He has extensive experience dealing with the negative forms of sexuality but also recognizes that it is an essential part of humanity and is not inherently bad or harmful. Orgasmic Meditation, he notes, offers a direct path to engage with sexual arousal, but with the container that allows for the safety necessary for a therapeutic process.

We have come to think of trauma as a permanent condition,

that we "become traumatized" and are destined to carry this burdensome weight for the rest of our lives. But this idea of our experience as something to "manage" ignores the possibility that we can transform that experience into something new. Orgasm is accepting of all, and arousal in the proper conditions allows us to integrate experiences that may otherwise feel unsafe. Without this integration, we often react in ways that unintentionally reify the pattern we wish to escape. But what if these labyrinthine conditions and preprogrammed reactions could instead serve as fuel for the creative fire wishing to express through us? After speaking to OM practitioners who described their personal, transformational experiences with a variety of histories related to trauma, Dr. Kriegman sought to learn more.

The result was a phase I clinical trial to determine whether Orgasmic Meditation could serve as a safe and effective intervention for people suffering from PTSD. It was a line of inquiry similar to recent studies that aimed to treat PTSD and other maladies using psychedelics—particularly those capable of inducing mystical or profoundly meaningful subjective experiences.[16] Dr. Vivian Siegel's research had shown that OM was capable of producing mystical experiences for its practitioners. The inquiry started in the phase I trial that will continue into phase II and III is: If meaningful relief from trauma could be found in the mystical state, could OM be a safe way to heal those traumas through the body itself?

Thirteen pairs of individuals, of whom at least one of the two suffered from PTSD, joined the study. They learned to OM using the OM App online with minimal interaction with the

16. Kwonmok Ko, Gemma Knight, James J. Rucker, *et al.* "Psychedelics, Mystical Experience, and Therapeutic Efficacy: A Systematic Review," *Frontiers in Psychiatry* 13 (2022), https://doi.org/10.3389/fpsyt.2022.917199.

researchers and engaged in the practice a minimum of twelve times over the four weeks of the study.

The results were remarkable. Of the participants who initially scored above the threshold of a PTSD diagnosis, the average score of their trauma assessment dropped 47 percent. No one dropped out of the study, and in fact OM was evaluated as a 4.9 out of 5 for "safety." Participants reported that they felt less isolated, less anxious, and less sad after engaging in OM. Depression and anxiety measures improved significantly. The resounding response was that OM created a safe space for intimacy and emotional connection[17]—all without the negative side effects associated with medication and reexposure therapy or the slowness of yoga or traditional meditation.

There is more research to be done, but these findings point toward the potential of OM as a complementary, body-based practice that may help those who struggle with traditional treatments. Providing access to a safe, healing experience with clearly defined boundaries and no expectation of performance allows us to access our spiritual circuitry. This is one especially powerful mechanism through which OM practitioners can experience healing.

Finding Optimal Arousal

The results of Dr. Kriegman's study were stunning and echoed the findings of Dr. Prause and Dr. Siegle's research that demonstrated people with histories of trauma were having remarkable experiences in Orgasmic Meditation. Prause and Siegle had

---

17. Daniel Kriegman, Rachel Pelletier, Caroline Griggs, and Caryn Roth, "Phase 1 Clinical Trial on Orgasmic Meditation (Om): Assessing Safety and Feasibility as a Meditation Practice for Individuals with PTSD," SSRN, December 9, 2024, https://doi.org/10.2139/ssrn.5033744.

hypothesized that it was the consistent structure of OM that allowed people to feel safe to choose the practice of OM and have these experiences. Indeed, participants of Dr. Kriegman's study rated their feelings of safety in OM at an average of 4.9 out of 5, and the marked decreases in symptoms related to PTSD made it clear something real is happening in OM.

> **Optimal arousal** is the ideal balance point of sensation and attention in Orgasmic Meditation practice, where we exist with maximum openness to and capacity for transformative experiences without pushing into climax or overwhelm.
>
> Rather than escalating toward climax, optimal arousal is achieved through a *resonant stroke*—an attuned, cocreated rhythm between the stroker and strokee. Adjustments in speed, pressure, direction, or the location of the stroke on the clitoris fine-tune the experience to match the body's natural energetic state. This process allows awareness to become fully engaged in vibrant detail, without exceeding the threshold where sensation becomes overwhelming or contractions set in.
>
> In this state, traditional labels of "good" and "bad" dissolve, and sensation is experienced in its raw, unfiltered form.

But what? That was the question turning over in Dr. Siegle's mind when we met in the summer of 2024. Dr. Siegle is primarily an emotion researcher whose work spans across depression, PTSD, and autism. In addition to OM, he has researched human physio-emotional response across a wide variety of experiences from laboratory settings to the thrills of a haunted house or the intensity of BDSM play.

Traditional models of emotion usually depict feelings on a simple two-dimensional grid: emotions running from positive to negative along one axis, and arousal on the other, signifying intensity. But the science wasn't lining up. In a recently published paper, Dr. Siegle saw that "nearly the same networks were activated for savoring and rumination, primarily including the brain's default, executive, salience, and memory networks."[18] Whether we are thinking about things we enjoy or things we worry about, the same parts of our brain are triggered. Like the pistons of an engine firing, regardless of whether we have the car in drive or reverse.

If our emotions worked the way they are laid out on the grid, then positive emotions like 'happy' would lie on one side and negative emotions like 'sad' would be on the other side, and that would be it. And while that may describe a good portion of our lived experience, we're all familiar with common outliers. "Cute aggression" is a familiar, if confusing, combination of emotions. When seeing that kitten or baby all of a sudden inspires our muscles to clench and the urge to bite or squeeze, are these positive feelings or negative? It may be that the map does not quite encompass the terrain.

As intensity increases, positive emotions may rise all the way to "ecstasy," and negative emotions could increase to "horror." If we were to plot those positions on the "emotion grid," they should maintain their distinct separateness. But that's not what Dr. Siegle was seeing. At high levels of arousal, the usual reports that clearly distinguish between "good" and "bad" begin to blur or even cross over from one to the other. Suddenly, the seemingly "negative" experiences people *enjoy* began

18. Benjamin O. Brandeis, Greg J. Siegle, et al., "Subjective and Neural Reactivity During Savoring and Rumination," *Cognitive, Affective, & Behavioral Neuroscience* 23 (2023): 1568–1580, https://doi.org/10.3758/s13415-023-01123-2.

to make sense—whether that's a jump scare at a haunted house or a spanking scene in BDSM. Similarly, the "emotional shock" that can result from high-arousal experiences like sudden news, good or bad, could be modeled by a continuum where extremely high arousal loops back to extremely low arousal without traveling through the usual intermediary states like "vaguely interested" or "bored."

Dr. Siegle began to imagine other models for the landscape of our emotions. Maybe the flat grid on the wall would be more accurate as a diamond or a triangle? Noting how brain regions like the amygdala and insula, which are involved in processing both reward and punishment, respond similarly during these elevated states, he imagined the map rolled into a tube where positive and negative might loop from one into the other at the extremes. Possibly a globe with positive and negative feelings clearly defined at the equator but less distinct as you near the North Pole? In the high-arousal zone, even sensations we would label as "pain," at the right intensity and within the correct relational framework, could be experienced as intensely pleasurable.

Combining these observations, Dr. Siegle settled on a model he referred to as the "emotion donut," which allowed for continuous loops of both emotional valence (positive and negative) and high and low arousal. This model may explain what Orgasmic Meditation practitioners refer to as "optimal arousal." Rather than simply stroking harder and faster in a rush toward climax (which, in Dr. Siegle's model, would be akin to falling through the inner donut hole from high arousal to low arousal), OM practitioners aim for a "resonant" stroke—an attuned, co-created experience between two people. Strokees may request a faster or slower stroke, more or less pressure, and strokers tune their attention to the connected, felt experience of stroking. In doing so, both stroker and strokee are able to reach a balance of arousal that absorbs the attention without going over into sexual climax.

It may be that this "optimal arousal" is exactly the place where the rigid labels of good and bad, as well as our predetermined reactions, can come undone. In a setting like OM that is conducive to safety and exploration, it may prove that *arousal* is the key element that allows us to pierce through the valence of good and bad, right feelings and wrong, into the raw experience as the full, complex beings we naturally are. The power to enter the space of possibility and rewrite our narratives is available within us. This is the power of orgasm.

The Power of Connection

OM is unique in that, unlike most meditative techniques, it's a partnered practice. As brain scans show, this creates additional benefits for participants.

Specifically, Dr. Newberg noted activity in the insula and the precuneus, which are both linked to social interactions.[19] The insula not only helps us perceive our own feelings, it plays a large role in empathy by helping us understand *others'* emotions. The precuneus helps us maintain a sense of self, but it also assists us in relating to others. As Dr. Newberg describes, this combined activity can result in the creation of stronger social bonds between individuals. OM enhances neural pathways involved in human relating, fostering deeper connection and emotional well-being. In life, we begin to open to the ability to have positive relationships and see others as a potential source of pleasure and healing rather than of pain.

Additionally, Dr. Newberg noted a type of activity in the temporal lobe that indicates it's the specific combination of

19. Newberg, *Sex, God, and the Brain,* 76.

sexual stimulation and intense focus that enables such profound experiences. Further, scans showed that OM doesn't just excite or inhibit certain areas of the brain, it is also associated with how these areas work together. And because changes were evident *even after the sessions had concluded*, these findings suggest that such alterations endure away from the nest and out in the real world.

And that is precisely what participants report. One woman who had experienced childhood trauma described, "OM made me realize that I actually could feel. There was nothing wrong with my body. . . . That actually opened up more connections in my life."[20]

Another OM practitioner who had experienced PTSD from military service said, "Different layers started peeling off. I remember walking away like the whole weight of the world had been lifted off my shoulders."

His wife reported a similar experience, saying OM "went straight down to the root" and helped to alleviate "baggage that I carried with me since the time I was a child."

The veteran added that the healing he experienced as a result of OM has made him a better partner and father. Dr. Prause and Dr. Siegle studied whether OM would increase feelings of closeness among partners, whether they were romantic partners or not. (Among the 125 couples who participated, roughly half participated with their romantic partner.) Overall, OM did result in greater feelings of closeness among partners; interestingly, even more so between those who were not romantically involved.

Additionally, both men and women reported a greater overall sense of self-awareness, which they said had a positive

20. "The Science of Orgasmic Meditation: A Path to Deeper Connection and Joy," virtual lecture, posted December 21, 2023, by IOM Foundation, YouTube, 44:42, https://www.youtube.com/watch?v=mLnktDzkYk8.

impact on their romantic partnerships. This echoes Dr. Newberg's insights about brain activation in areas associated with both the self and the self in relationship to others.

Women reported increased physical sensation, awareness of others, and self-confidence, and an increase in their overall quality of communication and sex life. Men indicated that OM also increased their sense of confidence, awareness of others, physical sensations, and sexual awareness. They, too, reported improved communication and quality of sex.

One of the most powerful aspects of OM is that it helps us to *co-regulate*. In a very real sense, our nervous system tunes to those around us. "There's certainly evidence that human brains do resonate with each other—especially when they're in communication and connected," Dr. Newberg notes. "For example, when you're sitting in a house of worship and people are singing a hymn, there's a rhythmic element, and everyone gets entrained into that rhythm."[21]

This is especially true in such a directed, intentional practice as OM. A feedback loop exists between the practitioners where both partners' attention is on the point of contact and the sensations that arise. That shared activity can affect areas of the brain, including parts of the parietal lobe, which is responsible for sensory information. Many OM practitioners report they experience the same sensations in their bodies at the same moment as their partner. As practitioners increase their practice, they can take this experience into the world outside of the nest.

As one male practitioner noted, "Honing my sensitivity in the OM container directly influences how sensitive I can be

---

21. "The Impact on the Brain from Partnered Practices like OM with Dr. Andy," virtual lecture, posted January 30, 2025, by Institute of OM, Vimeo, 7:56, https://vimeo.com/1051934389/e730920b6f.

in all other areas of my life. Relating with women became less scary, while noticing how people are feeling around me became the norm, and being able to pick up on the signals of my own body became my main way of navigating through daily life. The more I stay connected to my strokee, the more deeply I'm able to connect with myself."

When we merge with our everyday environment as we do in the practice of OM, it confers the experience of intimacy. It's not just about the other person, or even ourselves. We instead become intimate with all of life because we have dissolved the barriers that kept us from connection.

This is more than metaphorical; it's represented in the correlated brain activity Dr. Newberg noted among the OM partners, most strongly seen in the insula and precuneus—regions especially involved in social processing. "This speaks to the idea that OM really focuses on a social, person-to-person connection," Dr. Newberg explained.

He continued: "[The insula and precuneus] help us understand how the self fits within the social framework of the world. When you say, 'I feel connected to X,' what we are designed to be connected to is each other. We're designed to be connected to our family members, a loved one, a mate, a child, or whoever. And when that connection is extrapolated to a group, to God, or to the universe, you get these expansive, expanded perceptions of the self in a social context. In fact, many people think about God in a social context, in terms of having a relationship with God." OM trains our strength of connection and intimacy—with ourselves, with our partner, and beyond.

One woman described the shock of this experience. At the end of a session, as she and her partner—who was not a romantic partner—described the sensations they had each felt, suddenly she looked at him and felt as if she could "see into his soul. And not only that," she added, "I felt him see me. . . . That intimacy was a feeling I'd been starving for, for so long. . . . What I was feeling wasn't falling in love. It actually had little to do with him. It was me experiencing pure, unadulterated connection with another human being." Indeed, something in her had opened, and that opening changed her immeasurably, and irrevocably.

In his book, *The Light Inside the Dark: Zen, Soul, and the Spiritual Life*, John Tarrant captures the process through which such transformations occur. He writes, "Attention is the most basic form of love: through it we bless and are blessed. When we attend to the interior life, we also connect with what surrounds us . . . And it is this inner connection that resolves the problem of who we are and makes us at home in the world."

Through the experience of oneness with all that is, and through the communion of loving attention, the questions we hold and the conflicts we imagine—all are resolved. We at once connect more deeply, more gently, and more powerfully with ourselves, *and* with the world beyond our boundaries, than we ever thought possible.

CHAPTER 3

What Stands Between
Us and Orgasm?

I n Chapter 1, I posed a question to you via the Sufi poet Rumi:
"Why do you stay in prison when the door is wide open?"
Now we come to examine what appears to stand in our way and
is obscured so thoroughly that it's difficult to see where the
blockage is, and where it isn't. That's because the blockage influences, at a nonconscious level, every aspect of how we interact with life. In this setup, it's difficult to even conceptualize
the idea of living in orgasm.

I have the same conversations with women again and again.
One particular friend has spent the last five years telling me
about her anxiety. It's always the same. She doesn't *know* why
she's struggling, but I do. The cause is *tumescence*. We have this
sediment inside of our systems that needs to be stirred up,
cleared out, and repurposed. When it's just left there, it forms
a mass inside us that restricts the flow of energy in such a way
that life starts to feel confounding and confusing, difficult to
navigate, a chore.

When we don't know it's tumescence that's causing this,
we believe we are trapped in and by our *symptoms*. If we could

only make these bad feelings stop, life would be better. So, we get diagnosed and medicated, all the while moving farther and farther from ourselves. From living in orgasm. So far, in fact, we can't even imagine a different way of being. The idea of existing in flow is difficult to picture.

The very word tumescence may conjure the image or sense of a tumor—a distorted mass that results from natural functions going awry. In many ways, that's exactly what this blockage is. At any given time, there are cells in our body that are distorted and would produce tumors if left unchecked. But in an environment of health, the body routinely destroys and digests these cells and there is no malignancy. Similarly, it's natural for tumescence to arise, but in health and in flow, we use its energy to fuel creativity. We clear out the sediment, opening our channels so the energy of orgasm can move through us freely.

To be clear, when I speak of unexpressed desire, I'm not referring only to sexual desire. When we experience any kind of arousal—that state when something inside us stands at attention—and we suppress that rising wave, the result is tumescence. The initiating impulse of that wave is desire. What causes arousal within us may be sexual in nature, but it may also be intellectual, physical, or spiritual. Whatever the nature of our arousal, there is often a counterforce that urges us to tamp it down or some aspect of our physical reality that creates space between our desire and its satisfaction. This is the space of creation. The poet John Keats described the strength to stay in this space of uncertainty as a person's *negative capability*, "being in uncertainties, mysteries, doubts, without any irritable reaching after fact and reason." The unmet desire is the fuel of creativity; a growing pile of kindling waiting for the spark of circumstance and cause to ignite a transforming conflagration.

The difficulty of tumescence is that it can grow so large and waterlogged that we become cut off from ourselves and the sensation of desire within us. The necessary heat to transform this blockage to fuel becomes greater and greater until we may sense it's better to live on this side of the wall and come to demonize anything that may rise to disturb or disrupt this concretized way of living. "That's bad!" some part of us thinks (or is explicitly told, or perceives through a gasp, furrowed brow, or smack across the face), and by extension, we label ourselves as bad, too. As our urge or desire is suppressed, shame arises in its place. On one level, it is the shame of our desire being judged or rebuffed, and on another, it is our own shame at trespassing against ourselves by suppressing the natural expression that arose within us.

Dr. Vivian Siegel, a geneticist at MIT, explains humans have a history of internalizing the belief that erotic impulses are inherently bad. Embedded in this belief is the idea that if we act on such impulses, we might lose affection, status, or safety. That feels threatening, so we do not respond to the impulse. This can happen on a conscious or nonconscious level. The result is tumescence. As she explains, "I think a lot of why there's so much tumescence in our society is that the erotic messages from our body are intensely shamed."[22] There is a deep and historical belief that the erotic impulse holds negative consequences for us. From the story of Eve to our high school sex-ed classes, we are warned about the dangers of sex and any step in that direction, down to the sensations within our own bodies.

22. Dr. Vivian Siegel, PhD, "The Science of Tumescence: What Your Body Is Really Telling You," virtual lecture, posted May 21, 2024, by Eros Platform, YouTube, 17:42, https://www.youtube.com/watch?v=H4QVihgpGjk.

Erotophobia is an unconscious, irrational fear of erotic impulses and sexual expression, deeply ingrained in societal conditioning. It operates on both a cultural and personal level, creating shame resulting in suppression and then disconnection from the body's natural erotic energy.

This fear is not limited to overt expressions of sexuality but extends to any form of embodied desire—whether creative, intellectual, or relational. Erotophobia teaches individuals, particularly women, that their erotic energy is dangerous or wrong, leading to the suppression of pleasure and self-expression.

One of the major consequences of erotophobia is tumescence, the buildup of suppressed erotic energy in the body. Rather than allowing energy to flow naturally, erotophobia forces it to stagnate. The result is a frustrating sense of being emotionally or spiritually blocked. This tension often compounds, and a variety of physiological or psychological ailments ensue. The suppression resulting from erotophobia particularly affects feminine power, as it disconnects women from their innate ability to attract and influence the world—a capacity rooted in the life-giving, erotic force.

Releasing erotophobia requires unlearning societal messages that cast erotic energy as dangerous, and reclaiming the ability to feel and express desire in an open, connected way. Through practices like Orgasmic Meditation, individuals can begin to dismantle these fears, restore flow, and reestablish their relationship with their own eroticism as a source of power rather than shame.

In the 1970s, psychologists introduced the term "eroto-phobia" to describe fear, aversion, or negative attitudes toward expressions of sexuality. Like other phobias, erotophobia is an irrational fear motivated by the unconscious. In his book, *The Politics of Lust*,[23] lawyer and individual liberty advocate John Ince actually describes homophobia as a specific expression of erotophobia. Whether referring to this phenomenon as "Puritanical," "anti-sex," or "sex-negative," they all point to the pervasive fear of sexual expression.

Gayle Rubin, often described as the founder of gender studies, noticed how the idea of sex triggers such intense sensations that people have a hard time accepting their own sexuality, let alone expressions of sexuality that don't align with their own preferences. In her revolutionary essay, "Thinking Sex,"[24] Rubin describes how social groups work to keep sexual expression contained within a "charmed circle" and see other forms of sexuality as lesser or in opposition to the privileged form.

She's speaking broadly. These reactions, value judgments, and resulting hierarchies aren't limited to any specific group, though whatever groups have the most social power leverage their views and preferences onto society as if they were the *one* way things should be. We can see the effects of erotophobia and the idea of the charmed circle in recent American history and the expansion of sexual freedom, from interracial marriages, the acceptance of sex out of wedlock, and the gay rights movement. Today, we find ourselves on the next cusp of the sexual revolution with the possibility to unleash a feminine sexuality rooted in orgasm. In this form of sexuality, erotic

23. John Ince, *The Politics of Lust* (Prometheus, 2005).
24. Gayle Rubin, "CHAPTER 9: Thinking Sex: Notes for a Radical Theory of the Politics of Sexuality," *Culture, society and sexuality : a reader* (1998): UCL Press, https://doi.org/info:doi/.

impulse itself is celebrated and nurtured into its desired expression. While previous movements have taken their banner to bring certain expressions of the erotic within the charmed circle, we aim to turn our attention from the surface appearances of permission and acceptance, down to the roots of what wishes to rise and what rises to block it.

From the day we're born, women are told that we need to withhold our sexuality. We have to cross our legs, and we have to act ladylike. Everything around sex gets shut down, and we're not supposed to talk about it, or be sexual in any way. In the same way, men get all of their empathy shut down. Later, women are trying to get men to be more empathetic and men are trying to get women to be more sexual. The two don't often meet. This is one byproduct of OM. She gets to own her sexuality in a way that contradicts everything she's learned, and he gets to own his compassion in a way that contradicts everything he's learned. It's a very deep shift.

Tumescence often feels (physically or energetically) like a swelling or a buildup of pressure. If by now you're thinking, "Story of my life!" you're right. It's the story of all our lives, because no one is without tumescence, though it varies in size and severity. As we learn to work with our tumescence, we begin to recognize impulse suppression in its early stages when our tumescence is simply a pebble. We can easily undertake practices to convert its energy and restore flow. To return to or maintain the state of orgasm.

Left unaddressed, tumescence—this inflammation of the psyche—wreaks havoc. But while moving it is anything but easy, there's a silver lining and a strong motivation for undertaking this journey of openness. To paraphrase the Gospel of Saint Thomas: That which you do not express will destroy you, but that which you do can be your salvation. We can also think of tumescence as stored energy. As such, what's inside it has tremendous potential to fuel us. But we must learn not only how to access it, but to expand our capacity in a way where we can deal skillfully with what is released so we can direct this energy toward serving it.

Tumescence, derived from the Latin *tumere*, meaning "to swell," refers to the accumulation and blockage of suppressed desire or emotional energy within the body. It arises when erotic energy is redirected away from its natural flow, either consciously or unconsciously. This unprocessed energy builds up like plaque in an artery, creating tension and stagnation. A feeling of dissatisfaction and discomfort persists.

When left unchecked, tumescence negatively impacts psychological, spiritual, and physical well-being. It manifests as irritability and a sense of being "stuck" in life. At advanced stages, diagnoses and sickness develop.

Unlike orgasm, which is a continuous flow of vital energy, tumescence is a congestion that prevents this energy from being fully expressed. It feeds on itself, creating patterns of complaint, resentment, and reactivity, leading to exhaustion and emotional disconnection. Tumescence, too, is a raw energy that can be transformed by converting it to dynamic flow through attention and deliberate practice.

The Nature of Tumescence

If this concept sounds at all familiar to you, that's because like any real truth, it's found expression via many different tongues. In Buddhism, it's similar to *suffering*. Eckhart Tolle refers to our *pain body*—a similar concept, yet what Tolle conjures is a force that's, in essence, outside of us, while tumescence builds and resides within. Writers and other creatives (though in fact, aren't we all creatives?) might simply call it a block. All describe essentially the same thing. It's *that thing* you can't seem to get past, and what holds you back or makes you feel bloated. It's as if our system has developed a contortion, or a kink, much like a garden hose that's gotten twisted. Subsequently, if water—the energy of orgasm, the impulse to express—moves toward the constriction, pressure builds.

> One of my patients at the cancer care facility described a feeling of having a kind of bubble sitting in her body. I was taken aback when she said that because I knew what she meant. I'm familiar with that feeling of a bubble in my body. Especially at times when I need to express something, but I feel scared; it's like I can't access what's inside that bubble. The bubble is keeping me separated from it.

The blockage begins and builds any time we suppress an instinct to speak, to create, to delight in the sensuality of the world—including our body—to acknowledge and express our purpose. It's also there when we feel nothing at all. Just as muscle tissue that holds too much tension for too long first becomes tender and sensitive, then adhered, then totally numb as blood can no longer move through it, eventually becoming necrotic. Fortunately, just like with the garden hose that's taken on a twist, it doesn't take a lot to heal—meaning a lot of doing, of effort-ing, of pushing, shoving, or cajoling. Our body is naturally inclined toward healing. In some way, health is always present, we need only remove the barriers.

Instead, we focus on "fixing." Consider another metaphor of the body. A common approach to massage therapy is to locate the problem and to try to make it stop problem-ing. To apply pressure, to knead and to stretch in an effort to get the tissue to do what you want it to do, which usually has less to do with true healing and is more about making the discomfort stop. When we're really committed, we tell the therapist to go for it! To dig in. We can take it! They apply their will to the tissue, trying to force the result we want (and in the process can actually cause tearing or inflammation or nervous system disruption from which we will now also have to heal). In the end, we've never actually addressed what caused the issue in the first place, and so we'll find our way back to the table again and again.

Some modalities of therapy rely not at all on the therapist actively *doing* anything. There's little to no physical manipulation, only gentle holding of the body at key places while attending and witnessing. In biodynamic craniosacral therapy, for instance, the practitioner observes the body's *tides*—the movement of the cerebrospinal fluid as it rolls, wavelike, from the base of the spine to the brain, and back again. They simply notice the flow and take note of *inertial fulcrums*—spots where the flow is interrupted or changes course. The simple act of holding a safe container and providing nonjudgmental attention creates an atmosphere where the client is free to experience "still points," where the body's own healing intelligence can exercise its wisdom. Instead of targeting dis-ease, such approaches locate and support the health that is present, no matter how faint or obscured. The combined energy of the client's and practitioner's attention is directed at simply noticing what is and supporting the body as it seeks to restore health. This is similar to the container and relationship between the stroker and strokee in the practice of OM—neither exerts any particular effort to "make something happen," but instead are connected within a shared experience, allowing what wants to occur naturally rise to the surface.

Depending on how tumesced we are when we begin to convert what's been stored, it can re-trigger the initial feeling that we suppressed and we can experience that shame, that discomfort, that anger, and so on all over again—sensations that may or may not have a story attached to them. These emotions or body sensations act like an unwelcome house guest who stops to say goodbye on their way out the door. We may dread the interaction, the conversation, but if we can stay with it, eventually it will pass and we will have our home back to ourselves. Yet our guest hasn't exactly left; it has transformed into available energy. We can experience this as a sense of vitality or a sense of being fueled or resourced.

So OMing, while it engages our sexuality and our arousal, doesn't always feel good in the conventional sense, though often it does. Eventually, we learn to welcome whatever arises, including discomfort, recognizing that freedom is on the other side. There are no shortcuts, and our avoidance will eventually reveal to us that there is no way around, only through. If we try to skip past what feels unpleasant, we'll find diminishing returns from our practice.

There was a woman who, by common measures, would be considered highly accomplished—she'd founded a nonprofit aimed at social justice, was well respected by her peers, highly educated, and so on. She wished to confront and transform the trauma she knew was dwelling inside her from her childhood. Through lots and lots of *work*, she had become aware that the trauma—her tumescence—was causing her to doubt herself, obscuring her awareness, and generally making things difficult. While she could still *do* and *achieve* a lot, everything was an uphill battle. Very little seemed like it came easily or naturally. As a result, she was exhausted.

Nervous system expert Irene Lyon might say that she was "hitting the gas while the brakes were on."[25] Rather than figure out how to release the brake, as so many of us do, she simply hit the gas harder, hoping to outrun or break through the resistance she felt.

Having exhausted talk therapy and other more conventional approaches, like many in our modern era, she sought out the assistance of an indigenous shaman, and multiple sessions with psychedelics ensued. Yet each time she entered the space inside herself, traversing down and down, she ran into a gatekeeper who declared, in true *Lord of the Rings* fashion, "You shall not pass!" Over and over, he barred her passage. Again and again, she approached the door and was denied admittance.

So she turned to the approach that had been so effective for her in the external world— she attempted to storm the barricades. "Let me in!" she demanded, but still the gatekeeper refused.

From the viewpoint of OM, what the guard was blocking access to was her tumescence, and also her vitality. While it frustrated her, it wasn't "bad" that she was kept from accessing it. In fact, there was an intelligence there, for even the tumescence knew she did not yet have the tools to deal effectively with what

25. Irene Lyon, "Functional Freeze Explained," posted January 8, 2023, by Irene Lyon, YouTube, 24:52, https://www.youtube.com/watch?v=-qPCzzn-uQA&t=1326s.

was inside Pandora's box. She had not yet trained her attention and did not have the ability or capacity to ride the tsunami that would have been released with the gate's sudden opening.

Distraught, she searched for a distraction. She became a voracious reader of romance novels. She grew obsessed with the stories, even avoiding her work to consume them, to try to fill that hunger caused by being cut off from herself. This made her even more ashamed, because not only was she "underperforming" at work, but also because a woman of *her intellect* and a *strident feminist* should not find pleasure in such insipid and demeaning storylines.

Addiction expert Anna Lembke once succumbed to this same form of distraction.[26] Lembke says it was beyond her that she, as a clinical psychiatrist and a professor at renowned Stanford University, and mother of two, would fall prey to such stories. Yet, there she was, staying up all night devouring them. As Lembke said, she later recognized that she was using the romance novels as a means of escaping her own reality. The titillation they provided was particularly effective at hooking her into a fantasy world where she didn't have to deal with the challenges of life beyond their steamy pages.

As Lembke described it, no matter how many books she devoured, nothing satisfied her. She always craved more. This is what tumescence does. It forms a bolus that blocks nourishment and satisfaction. We are bloated yet starving. In time, that hunger becomes completely nonconscious. This is why the swelling can not only look like binging (on food, alcohol, or other drugs, but also on green smoothies, sprouts, and supplements) but also denial (of food, of pleasure, of anything we feel we haven't "earned the right to").

---

26. https://www.annalembke.com, accessed January 27, 2025.

While Lembke described the challenges of reality, we might describe what we seek to escape as *the challenge of being human*. After all, the human experience is messy, and our solution for the problem of being human is to *deny* that we're human. Meaning, we deny our desire. We suppress all that we perceive or are explicitly told is unwanted, unattractive, unbecoming. But still, it beats like the "Telltale Heart" beneath the floorboards.

Our greatest fear in life becomes that someone else will discover the evidence we've stashed beneath the surface. We contort ourselves and our lives in all kinds of ways to try to obscure it from others, but still we hope to be discovered.

We bury what is unpalatable or inconvenient—our hunger, desire, yearning, and even love—but it doesn't go away. Instead, hidden in the dark, it becomes distorted and deranged. When our tumescence is triggered, it comes out as outrage, upset, or anger. But those initial natural and even beautiful impulses are still in there, and we can still access and liberate them.

In its advanced stages, tumescence takes on a self-protective mechanism. It is a master at diversion, distraction, and camouflage. But no matter how large or advanced it is, and no matter how developed its security systems, tumescence does have a master, and that master is the *energy of orgasm*. Tumescence is powerless against the flow of life energy, which is the only force capable of unwinding all that binds us.

Six Levels of Tumescence

One way we can think of tumescence is as heightened energy with a contraction. Our *level* of tumescence increases when we contract around the contraction. If we start to panic and then we panic about the panic, we get an extra contraction. If we get positive attention for the panic, we contract there as well, and suddenly we have three contractions—we are at the third level of tumescence.

Here, roughly, are the six stages:

0. In stage zero, there is no tumescence, only pure, consistent flow. Impulses arise within us, we become aroused, and that energy immediately repurposes into creative expression of whatever form. In this space, our bandwidth is wide open. It's easy to work with whatever happens and we feel happy to do so. We see clearly that all things—even if they seem bad or negative—hold energy that we can use in service of life. We are like the aikido master who can receive energy from an attacker, and instead of meeting force with force, lovingly direct it.

1. In this stage, our energy heightens and there is a slight contraction. I have a friend who has a distinct memory of standing in the stairwell of her elementary school when she was in second grade, then seeing an older girl walk by. A thought popped into her mind, unbidden. "She's so pretty. I want her to be my girlfriend!" Immediately her mind constricted. *"That's not right!"* something hissed. This being rural America in the early 1980s, she didn't have a concept of "gay" or "lesbian," but still she had an inherent knowing that her impulse was "wrong." The cultural message of the time and region had permeated her psyche.

2. Next, we notice the contraction and we contract around it by judging not only what has arisen, but our reaction to it. Following from the previous example, as an adult, this woman might notice her own "internalized homophobia" and scold herself for it.

3. The next layer is the contraction around the contraction, and around the initial contraction. With each additional layer, the nesting doll within us becomes more difficult to open and that initial suppressed impulse becomes harder to access. As layers are added, we do not even see or remember how or when the suppression began, or what impulse moved us in the first place. Often the very start of our tumescence was in childhood, possibly even when we were preverbal.

4. Level four is the first level of diagnosis. We begin to experience *symptoms*, both psychological and physical, resulting from our constriction.

5. In stage five, our symptoms drive us to seek help, often of the medical variety. The result is a prescription for antacids, anti-anxiety meds, antidepressants, sleep aids, and so on.

6. In this stage, actual sickness occurs as we experience some kind of breakdown or overwhelm.

In the first two levels, our tumescence still has a suppleness to it, such that a friend who senses our constriction might bring it to our attention. We're able to hear them and see the evidence of what they say, and as a result, engage in some activity (practice OM, take a bath, meditate, go for a walk, engage in a creative activity) to loosen the constriction and restore flow. In later stages, however, we see any attempt to identify the tumescence (a friend noticing our "touchiness" or the fact our shoulders are in our ears and our jaw is clenched) as an indictment or insult. We become reactive. The tumescence has begun to protect itself.

There was a couple I was working with recently who'd been together for a long time. She had bladder cancer. She'd been at the facility for six months, which is a long time—most people are there for about six weeks. But she was getting a lot of care there, plus her husband was really engaged, giving her a lot of special attention. But while he was so attentive to her, I noticed she never responded in kind. She never acknowledged him or reciprocated.

We were talking about how we hadn't been able to move the needle on her cancer, and so I asked her a deeper question. I asked, "What's your secondary gain in having this cancer in your bladder?" In other words, what are you getting out of it?

Eventually, it came out. She said that during the course of their entire 47-year marriage, she felt as if she'd been raped. She didn't mean that her husband had literally forced himself on her, but that she'd never been a full-body *yes*. She'd never experienced that. And she'd reached a breaking point. Having cancer and being in the facility, she was finally receiving what she'd wanted all along. Care. Empathy. Intimacy.

I recalled that during my first meeting with this couple, one of the husband's first questions had been, "When can she have sex?" He wasn't insistent about it, but it was clear that sex was a priority for him. So there's that classic setup where she's wanting him to be more empathetic and he's wanting her to be more sexual. There was all that tumescence around things that had been pushed down or pushed away. It wasn't a coincidence that she had cancer in her genital area.

For me, that's where my OM practice came in—being able to hold that space with them where they could acknowledge their love for each other, but also her anger at him, and her recognition that she didn't know any other way to handle the situation than to just give in to his desires.

The key to healing is expression, but as we move from stage zero to six, we become more rigid and inflexible, less willing to express ourselves. Our desire for clinging increases. This can look like searching for a savior, for romance (or romance novels), and so on. We look outside of ourselves to ease or resolve our suffering, but what we reach for only amplifies it, and further distances us from ourselves. In this space we have a tendency to grab for the negative and push away the positive. Everything seems personal, and we attach to the outcomes of situations in an overactive way. We're unable to release our grip on what comes next.

A key structure involved in these processes is the vagus nerve. The longest of our cranial nerves, it consists of approximately 160,000 fibers that run from the brainstem to the gut.[27] The vagus nerve controls the parasympathetic functions of our heart, lungs, and digestive tract and influences everything from our immune system to our mood, helping to regulate our body's

27. Wikipedia contributors, "Vagus nerve," *Wikipedia, The Free Encyclopedia*, https://en.wikipedia.org/w/index.php?title=Vagus_nerve&oldid=1282011519 (accessed March 24, 2025).

inflammatory response. It also plays a major role in our ability to self-regulate, and to co-regulate with others.

When we suppress our impulses (which, again, typically starts when we are very young), our vagus nerve is affected. Our nervous system becomes dysregulated.[28] As we continue to suppress unwelcome impulses, this pattern persists and our tumescence builds. We grip harder and harder in an effort to both suppress ourselves and to control the world around us in an attempt to feel safe. When we are heavily tumesced, we feel that something is always wrong.

As we grip, our parasympathetic system—the part of our autonomic nervous system that functions as the "brakes"—engages in a way that's not supportive of our health, or our ability to connect with others. Instead of performing its rest-and-digest functions, it locks us into *functional freeze*. We are able to function in life, but as Irene Lyon characterizes it, "the cost of doing business is very high."[29] This is the idea I mentioned earlier of driving while the brakes are on. It's when our sympathetic system is excited, yet at the same time our freeze mode is activated, locking parts of us down. Life is happening, but we're unable to move with it freely. We may perceive that we're going with the flow, because we're forcing movement, but inside there is resistance. This is where "syndromes" emerge.

As all this is happening, the body also armors itself, generating chronic patterns of involuntary tension, which not only causes physical discomfort and ailments, but also dampens or blocks our ability to express ourselves and our emotions. In this state, our perceptions of our inner and outer worlds are altered

---

28. Kathy L. Kain & Stephen J. Terrell, *Nurturing Resilience: Helping Clients Move Forward from Developmental Trauma,* (North Atlantic Books, 2018).
29. Irene Lyon, "Functional Freeze Explained," *Irene Lyon* (blog), January 8, 2023, https://irenelyon.com/2023/01/08/functional-freeze-explained-2/.

(for example, when we are hypervigilant to potential threats). Our interoception—our ability to sense our internal state or perceive internal processes—is numbed or impeded, and our kinesthetic awareness is impaired. We literally cannot move confidently or freely in the world.

Our high-tone dorsal vagal response kicks in because we lack the flexibility to approach or respond to life in a nuanced manner. It's on or it's off.[30] When something requires more bandwidth to deal with than we have available (because it is all being consumed by our tumescence), we easily go into overwhelm. Something brushes against our tumescence, triggering all that is inside it. We have a deep body-based response and clunk into freeze mode.

Yet, as we convert our tumescence, more bandwidth becomes available. We gain access to the resources and develop skill such that we can interact more gracefully with life's agitations. Eventually, they are no longer agitations, they are simply part of life, and at some point we can even welcome them.

When we slow down into our freeze, it's an attempt to self-protect. If we had more internal dynamism, the tumescence would dissolve. Sometimes this slowdown appears more like mania than freeze. This hyperactivity and lack of focus is the result of our slowed metabolism (both literally and figuratively). It is a *frenzied* slowness, which keeps us locked out of our naturally dynamic core. When we encounter a stimulus, it may be triggering or, at a lower level of tumescence, merely agitating or insulting. At an even lower level, we can laugh about it. (Pro tip: The harder it is to laugh, or to play, the more tumesced you are.)

For women, there is perhaps nothing more shameful than admitting we have desire. We would rather stay in deprivation

---

30. Kain & Terrell, *Nurturing Resilience*.

than acknowledge desire or let in the energy of orgasm. Women keep themselves in levels four through six when we don't admit we have desire. Were we to allow in the energy of orgasm, which is always seeking us—as Rumi said, "What you seek is seeking you"—we would have access to the internal dynamism that would transform the tumescence. Instead of running away from desire and living in complaint and unhappiness, we would be able to bring ourselves down on the tumescent scale, coming back into flow.

In the decades since I became a physician, I've worked with countless women who've said in some way that they've never experienced a healthy, positive relationship with sex or their sexuality. When I asked one patient in her early fifties about her sex life, her answer was, "I'm past that. I don't do that anymore." This was not an old woman.

So many women say they are happy to reach a point where they don't have to "bother" with sex anymore. I noticed that, often, the older a woman was, the smaller the speculum I'd have to use. In a physical way, they were losing elasticity, but that was coming from a mental place, as well.

To me, saying you don't want sex in life is like saying no to life itself. But we have to go through a process of opening in order for that to shift. For us to come into contact with and not be ashamed of our desire anymore.

As Dr. Vivian Siegel explains, humans have a range of inherent drives.[31] What evolution selects for is whatever will advance our ability to successfully procreate. On a deep biological level, everything from nurturing behavior to aggression is geared to help us reproduce. Our erotic drive is part of this, but you might also think of it more broadly like a creative drive, whether we create children, works of art, the way our genius expresses itself in the kitchen or the board room or anywhere else. In a very real way, we are designed to channel the creative energy of the universe. When we suppress an erotic impulse–whether it's wanting to hug someone or express our anger with them—we generate a cascade of internal responses. We actually suppress some of the same drives that are designed to keep us alive, such as hunger. We might deprive ourselves of food or other forms of nourishment, or we may swing the other way and overindulge. In the process, we become disconnected from our body's natural wellness, and then, symptoms arise.

Siegel says that when something arises in your body and you interpret it negatively, "You would start disconnecting, doing what you can to separate from that sensation." You also take whatever actions are necessary to avoid that sensation so you don't have to experience it again. "I would say tumescence is a form of trauma—that it arises from disconnecting from a natural drive, perhaps because it's culturally inappropriate or for some other reason." Once the trauma becomes trapped within our cells, "it has the same effects as other kinds of trauma."

"But the great news," Siegel continues, "is that there are ways to access trapped energy, and OM is an amazing way to do that. It's one of the forces, one might argue, that's actually powerful enough to move this energy through the system."

---

31. Siegel, "The Science of Tumescence."

As we liberate this energy, we learn to reconnect with ourselves, with our desire. We begin to hear our body's messages. "I'm hungry," it says, and so we give it something nourishing to eat. Once we start listening and responding to our body's signals, our body learns to trust us again.

One of the most powerful signals our body gives us is a desire for connection. Again, this links to our deepest biological impulses. Life energy is the energy of creation and of connection. As Siegel explains, "There is within it a drive for a force that flows between and among people." And if you feel that flow starting, "then it's stopped by judgment or criticism, there's a recoiling." OM helps to clear tumescence and restore that flow.

Humans can self-regulate, as well as co-regulate. Our bodies and brains *speak* to one another. In this way, our tumescence is contagious. As is our clarity.

Tumescence feeds not only internally, draining our vitality, but also externally, by creating circumstances and provocations beyond our conscious will (making it feel or appear as if life is *happening to* us). It assumes both physical and emotional forms, looking to draw more energy toward itself. If we are in levels four through six, we may find ourselves surrounded by people who are also in these levels, who live with complaints, general malaise, and are often sick with something or other. In other words, there's a lot of *drama*. Likewise, when we're in levels one through three, we're liable to find ourselves surrounded by people in these levels—people who live with flow, dynamism, and clarity.

In our tumesced state, our critical mind goes into overdrive, and we direct this criticism not only to ourselves, but also to others. This is one way tumescence affects the collective. A woman goes to a restaurant, and when her entrée arrives, it isn't prepared to her exact specifications. Immediately she becomes furious. The server is shaken and ingests her anger. Later, when his partner leaves the cap off the toothpaste, he flies into a rage fueled by the anger-tumescence he ingested earlier. Our tumescence bumps into others and activates their tumescence.

When we are critical of others, it's an attempt to deflect attention from ourselves. When we're critical of ourselves, it's actually an attempt to bring ourselves down—to quiet the panic and soften the intensity we feel. But it only serves to increase the tumescence. Our tumescence becomes like a dog desperate to release its pent-up energy—it tries to run itself out so it can experience relief. But any release is only a temporary off-gassing of pressure, just enough that we don't explode. It's similar to how climax is no more than a temporary release of tension.

Conversely, the practice of OM creates a *deliberate conversion* of tumescent energy, a controlled release that directs it into something we can *use*.

Transforming Tumescence

We can think of sexual climax as an expulsion of energy, which is, in essence, energy wasted. As we practice OM, we learn how to release tension while increasing our attention. This doesn't just provide relief or *take the edge off*—it creates transformation. We don't merely feel better, we become a more complex human being, able to interact with life more richly and with flexibility and nuance. We develop a strength that isn't rigid, knowing that whatever comes, we can welcome and work with it. Because rigidity is fragility. Bruce Lee told his students to stay relaxed because their responses would be quicker and more skilled. When we're rigid, we're slow and stupid, more likely to get hurt.

If you're strong and supple when life shows up, then it's an adventure. But if not, that's when you feel the need for safety and self-protection—when you're cowering all the time, worrying what will happen next. When we coddle and cover our pain or suppress it, we lock our pain into place. Orgasm converts our pain into power.

Right around the time I started OMing, I left my job at the hospital where I'd been working, practicing standard Western medicine. I was in the midst of a divorce, and I'd saved up a good chunk of money for retirement. I decided, instead of just giving it to my husband for alimony, I'd do something for myself. I'd start enjoying my life. For five years, I took OM classes, I went on cruises, I learned to ski. And I danced—a lot. I'd always been a good dancer; growing up in New York, back then they didn't card so I'd go to the clubs. Suddenly it was like I could do all these things in my life that I couldn't do before. I could play. Because I was OMing, the lights were coming back on. I felt like I didn't have to hide all the time and could be myself. All the layers I'd piled on were coming off.

With OM, we develop our attention as we develop the system to convert the tumescence. This is what enables us to direct the energy that's released. It fuels us as we create. As our tumescence softens, it releases our power, and this power trains and becomes responsive to the attention. Our attention then takes on the power to animate. Prior to this, we may have had plenty of great ideas, but they had no fuel behind them. Or we may have had plenty of passion, but no way to direct it. Recall the words of Wendy Palmer: "Energy tends to go where there is the most excitement, most clarity, most intensity. . . . By focusing our attention, we can stabilize ourselves."[32]

Without the ability to focus our attention, when the energy or power is made available, we look to spend it as quickly as possible to return to our homeostatic state for fear we may become overwhelmed. But when we train power and attention together, over time, our efforts are no longer effortful, and we are fueled endlessly. There is an ease and an enjoyment to our doing because we have removed the blocks to what is natural— the energy of orgasm becomes free to move through us.

From this liberated state, we find the fulfillment our heart longs for by showing up in the lives of others. People no longer have to tiptoe around us, afraid of setting us off. While we are no longer hypervigilant or hyperactive, neither are we hyporeactive. We have the ability to fully inhabit ourselves, and from this space we nurture authentic connection with one another. Gone are the masks, and we are honest and open in how we show up in the world. We no longer display various versions of ourselves to suit the circumstances and keep us safe. We appear always as our whole self.

At their heart, issues in any relationship—whether at work, home, or elsewhere— revolve around tumescence. The solution is always connection. OM may be an individual practice, but it is not a solo practice, and that is very purposeful. We can't take ourselves out of control. Connection is transformative, and it takes us to places we cannot reach alone. The OM nest is a boundaried space. If we can be seen and felt by someone inside that safe container, we can take it into our life outside the nest. As a result, our relationships begin to transform, sometimes in a way that seems almost mystical or miraculous. In

32. Wendy Palmer, *The Intuitive Body: Discovering the Wisdom of Conscious Embodiment and Aikido* (Blue Snake Books, 2008).

alignment with this transformation in our relationships, our relationship with sex transforms as well. It, too, becomes not about scratching an itch; instead, it truly feeds us. It is a virtuous cycle. As our tumescence softens and our vitality is restored, we are free to enjoy and experience sex in richer ways. We can enjoy our partners more, we can enjoy food more, we can enjoy our being more. And as we listen to our desire, our tumescence transforms. As we drop back through the levels of tumescence, approaching zero, our health is restored.

As Stella Resnick writes in *The Pleasure Zone*, "The best thing about sensual pleasure is that it awakens us to the present moment. . . . The vividness of our experience takes us out of our heads where we can get lost in fiction and moves us into our bodies where we feel more fully alive."[33] Indeed, we *are* more fully alive. Positive sexuality has profound benefits for our quality of life—our ability to experience eudaimonia, a state of human flourishing—and our health. As research shows, when women have positive sexual experiences, our bodies rejoice, enjoying benefits such as lower blood pressure, improved heart health, improved immune system functioning, higher self-esteem, decreased depression and anxiety, a stronger libido, better sleep, and less physical and emotional stress.[34]

One study analyzing the connection between genital touch and cerebral development in women found greater development of the somatosensory cortex among women who had more frequent sex. In an article in the *Journal of Neuroscience*, a team of researchers—headed by German researcher Dr. Andrea J. J. Knop—writes, "This is compatible with the idea that the female genital field has capacity for structural plasticity depending on its

33. Stella Resnick, *The Pleasure Zone: Why We Resist Good Feelings & How to Let Go and Be Happy* (Conari Press, 1997), 193.
34. "The Benefits of a Healthy Sex Life," Center for Women's Health, accessed January 27, 2025, https://www.ohsu.edu/womens-health/benefits-healthy-sex-life.

use, commensurate with the general 'use-it-or-lose-it' principle of experience-dependent plasticity. . . . Cortical plasticity serves to enhance the efficiency of processing of behaviorally-relevant inputs and represents an adaptive response."[35] Yet we cannot access these myriad benefits if tumescence blocks us.

While the process of transforming our tumescence is simple, it is not easy. Sometimes it feels good. Sometimes it feels *really* good. At times, it feels uncomfortable. Sometimes excruciating. What, then, is our motivation to practice? Beyond reclaiming our vitality, our physical and mental health, and our ability to create, that is. The practice allows us to access the highest states of consciousness, where our intention for positive change in the world is purified and set. The intention is rooted in genuinely seeing the perfection of things as they are while also seeing where they want to evolve. We no longer need things to be a certain way, and are no longer so attached to feeling comfortable. We lose the drive to purposefully influence other people or shift how things are, knowing that when we operate from this consciousness, our very being and doing—our desire, our pleasure, our enjoyment, our expression, our creating—changes the world. We understand—*and are*—what it means to be fully human.

Joseph Campbell said, "I don't believe people are looking for the meaning of life as much as they are looking for the experience of being alive."[36] When we live in orgasm, we access our aliveness. We unleash ourselves on the world.

35. Andrea J. J. Knop, Stephanie Spengler, Carsten Bogler, *et al.* "Sensory-Tactile Functional Mapping and Use-Associated Structural Variation of the Human Female Genital Representation Field," *The Journal of Neuroscience* 42, no. 6 (2022): 1131-1140, https://doi.org/10.1523/JNEUROSCI.1081-21.2021.
36. Patrick Takaya Solomon, "Finding Joe," documentary, released September 30, 2011, posted March 19, 2020, YouTube, 01:19:12, https://www.youtube.com/watch?v=s8nFACrLxr0.

CHAPTER 4

Claiming Your Orgasm

"You're a sexist," I was once told, and by a man no less. I was living in a state of disempowerment, standing on my feminist soapbox preaching about the patriarchy, and here was this person—*this man*—telling me that between the two of us, *I* was the misogynist.

I sputtered my "How dare you!"s and looked to the women in the room for support. They looked back, unflinching. They knew he was right. The Gordian knot I found myself tangled in was one I'd constructed. Not men, *me*.

"The very thing that is your feminine power, you try to kill it," he said plainly as if stating something so obviously true that no one should require convincing. "You have the power. It's yours. But you won't take it."

He went on, describing in painful detail how I used my orgasm to get things—stuff, pleasure, attention. Or I pushed it away, demonizing it. I was speechless (a rare state). Everything I thought I knew about the relationship between men and women centered on the "fact" that men have made women into powerless objects with no volition.

And yet, I knew he was right in that way you do when real truth appears. Sometimes you sense it like a welcome warmth in your heart, but more often it grabs you by the intestines and twists, and that's what I felt in that moment. I was thoroughly unmoored. But by severing my attachment to the way I'd viewed the world, he had helped me take a first step toward liberation. I was now free to set down a real taproot, one that would deeply nourish me, that would help me come alive.

Up to that point I had spent all my energy—which felt like a finite resource because I was still caught in the *doing* trap—decrying my lowly status. Feeding the insatiable appetite of my victimhood while simultaneously starving myself of real sustenance—of love and connection. *Everything* felt wrong—and I always blamed it on someone else. It was impossible for me to trust or be trusted, and therefore to have any meaningful connections. Everything was surface, my every action and belief fueled by my righteousness. My judgment, my superiority, my withholding.

The moment he said it, my straw house burst into flames. But the fire didn't burn me. Instead, I let it thaw me. And as the blood began to rush back into places I hadn't sensed in years, or had never felt before, a torrent of pain shot through me. It was a sweet pain, the kind that comes when a slate is wiped clean, when the muses whisper in your ear, "*Now* you can begin," and you're flooded with knowing.

Because the energy of orgasm is neither withholding nor punitive. It is generous and benevolent. It *wants* you to be enlivened. Like a patient partner, it waits for you to return home. And the moment you lean toward it, you'll find it's been reaching for you all along.

Training the Nervous System

As I've said, the path may be simple, but it's anything but easy. You've got to get cracked open, like I was that day, so the energy can flow in. As Chinese medicine practitioner Thea Elijah says, "Healing happens when the love meets the pain and the love is in 51% or more voting majority."[37]

The fear is that you won't just be cracked but shattered. OM creates a container for your healing, like the cocoon in which the caterpillar quite literally comes apart. When her cells—cells that contain the blueprint for who the caterpillar is to become—are activated, she begins to reorganize herself. It is the struggle of breaking out of that shell, of beating her new wings again and again in an effort to set herself free that actually *makes* her strong enough to be in the world as her newfound self. Similarly, many women describe *claiming* themselves through the pain of childbirth, their own cells having been literally reorganized. In the midst of struggle, then surrender, they meet their own strength. But this isn't always the way it goes.

Navigating the path can be challenging, as there are countless traps in which our ego can ensnare us. For instance, as we begin to liberate our orgasm, we can easily attach it to something outside ourselves. To *someone.* If it feels *bad*, we blame someone or a situation for causing our discomfort, like how we lash out at anyone who touches our tumescence. If it feels *good*, we credit one near to us with our bliss, perhaps a partner or a teacher. As Thea Elijah observes, it's a common phenomenon that when we begin to heal, we engage in a kind of transference, crediting our practitioner or someone else with our

---

37. "About Thea Elijah," Perennial Medicine, accessed January 27, 2025, https://perennialmedicine.com/about-thea-elijah.

transformation.[38] Hence our obsession with gurus, with being a *follower* of someone we perceive as wiser than ourselves. But this golden projection disempowers us. In reality, *we* have initiated our own healing and liberation. The other may have played a supportive role, such as lending the energy of their attention to our process, but we are our own prime movers.

Reclaiming our orgasm isn't a path to ramble but a process of intentional training. This training includes guiding and showing our nervous system how to live in a state of openness and enjoyment of the journey of life rather than grasping and grabbing at momentary pleasure. All of this begins with attending to a basic sense of safety. As we discussed in the last chapter, when our nervous system is dysregulated, it cannot connect, and we cannot heal. So the process starts with resetting our system.

For many of us, a sense of true safety and security will feel like a revelation because we've never actually experienced it before. The sheer novelty can feel unsettling. The human brain often craves familiar patterns, whether positive or negative, healthy or dysfunctional, and so we can become unsettled in this new landscape and yearn for the way things were. For those who have experienced deep trauma, feeling a sense of *safety* can actually be triggering at first, especially if the traumatic event(s) occurred with someone or in a setting where they were supposed to be safe and protected.

Yet as clinical psychologist Edith Shiro writes in *The Unexpected Gift of Trauma*, we have the potential to engage with trauma as a lever for our own advancement. Shiro explains, we can use trauma and adversity to "leap forward." To not just return to the status quo, but to develop *beyond where we were before.* She writes that people who experience post-traumatic

---

38. Perennial Medicine, "About Thea Elijah."

growth view "trauma and adversity as possibilities for transformation, wisdom, and growth."[39] This is what we're describing when we talk about converting tumescence into fuel. But this takes time and practice.

It's been an awesome journey for me. I'm still learning how to be fully grateful for all of it. Ironically, now I find myself sometimes complaining about having too much. That's something that can happen in OM—all of these things start becoming available to you, becoming liberated, and you can almost feel a kind of overwhelm of abundance. That's when we have to increase our *having level*. We've become so accustomed to starving ourselves that we have to develop the ability to receive it all and just be with it.

Even for those of us without what we might describe as significant trauma, it's a process to learn to keep the energy of orgasm palpable and present without becoming overwhelmed or burning out, popping like a light bulb in a power surge. This is why we go slow, 15 minutes at a time. We're not trying to shatter a dam, we're trying to melt the ice, little by little.

Along the way, we learn to master the ability to modulate our power so that we can metabolize it. When this happens, we begin to experience a state of *eudaimonia*—that condition the Greeks described as "good spirit" (but modern translations reduce to "happiness"). When we're in good spirit, we are enlivened with the energy of life. With the energy of orgasm. It

39. Dr. Edith Shiro, *The Unexpected Gift of Trauma: The Path to Posttraumatic Growth* (HarperCollins, 2023).

animates all we do. Even if we encounter something that doesn't *feel* good, per se, we welcome it because we know it is purposeful. After all, everything is purposeful when we are in the state that Aristotle described as our *highest good*.[40]

Eudaimonia, an ancient Greek term meaning "good spirit" or "human flourishing," represents the highest state of well-being, authenticity, and fulfillment. It is not simply the pursuit of pleasure but the deep, ongoing realization of one's purpose, engagement in meaningful activities, and alignment with one's inner calling.

Eudaimonia naturally exists when we live in an orgasmic state. It emerges when a person operates from a space of presence and flow—where their energy is neither repressed nor squandered but continuously expressed in alignment with their deepest truth.

Unlike fleeting pleasure, which offers temporary satisfaction, eudaimonia is sustainable and ever-expanding. It is the skier having the perfect run, the artist lost in their work, or the mother fully immersed in love and connection with her children. It is a state of effortless engagement, where life is lived from a place of abundance rather than scarcity.

Through practices like Orgasmic Meditation, eudaimonia becomes not just an abstract ideal but an accessible, lived reality—one where pleasure, purpose, and deep human connection merge into a virtuous cycle of growth and vitality.

40. Duignan, B. "eudaimonia." *Encyclopedia Britannica*, March 1, 2025. https://www.britannica.com/topic/eudaimonia.

A friend of mine works with dogs commonly called pit bulls. The pit bull is largely thought to be a single breed of dog, when in reality, many mixes of bulldog and terrier can technically qualify as pit bulls, but in their "pure" state, most have similar temperaments. Women are similarly diverse, yet we share some powerful characteristics, both with one another and with these misunderstood canines.

As my friend explained, pit bulls were not bred for their *aggression*, but for their *devotion*. This is what prompts them to do precisely what their owner would have them do. They become what you train them to be—a vicious fighter, or a loving and loyal member of the family. My friend described the pit bull as "pure potential meets pure power." When they are aggressive, it is not because it's in their inherent nature to be so, but because we have abused their potential.

We, too, are where pure potential meets pure power. The force inside us can be trained to be similarly responsive. Through OM, we train receptivity, sensitivity, and the ability to surrender. When we can drop our attachment to our personal will, along with our judgments and preconceptions, we become truly responsive.

It's like ballroom dancers at the highest levels. The man can have the confidence and skill to lead, but the woman must also be a skillful follower, sensing his intention and being fully responsive so that their movements together are smooth and seamless. When it comes to dance, we would never look at the female partner and say, "Oh, she's so disempowered!" Instead, we admire her ability to so fully and expertly embody her role.

When we train our orgasmic capacity, we are not training our ability to *do more*, but to do less. To relax and release our grip. To accept. To receive. Our strength is in our suppleness and fluidity. Our sensing, our intuition, comes fully online and we can anticipate the next move just as it is arising. Using force invokes a counterforce. Instead, in this training, we learn to be open to what arises—responsive and at all times in flow.

So when I speak of training, what we are training is our receptivity. And what we must become receptive to is that which sits at the core of our tumescence—our long-suppressed desire.

The True Nature of Desire

One of the reasons we experience shame about our desire is that we have debased sexual power. We think of it as (or are told it is) a lesser power. Those shameful Greek goddesses always lured men to their doom with their sexuality, seducing them only to kill them. Or how the sirens crashed ships upon rocks. They also withheld sex as a punishment for some transgressions. Sex was a plaything, or a means of revenge.

Denigrating sexual power is denigrating women's power. We have learned to see our desire as inferior, a lesser or rudimentary kind of wanting fueled by our so-called lizard brain, or we moralize it and see it as dirty. As less than the force it is. We characterize it as wanting what we don't have, a yearning to fill an emptiness. When in truth, desire is no more (nor less) than fullness that longs to express itself. It is life *trying to happen* in all its richness.

Desire isn't specific. It's not about obtaining a thing—a person, a car, a ring—it is about allowing. It is a *wanting to be* more of who you truly are, in every moment.

Western interpretations of Eastern spirituality often hold that desire signals some kind of imbalance. That we should practice detachment and equanimity instead. That we should strive to be *calm*. In the Western conception of mindfulness, we believe that is the goal. We think our anger and every other unpalatable emotion needs to be extinguished, and so we take it to the mat, or the cushion, and engage in asana or sit in stillness until it abates. But it has not disappeared, it has simply joined with our tumescence, swelling it even further.

Instead, we can use the energy of our attention to *welcome* all that is, including and especially our more fundamental or "lower" feelings. Such philosophies characterize desire, itself, as base. Passion is to be avoided in favor of equanimity. And bodily sensations are to be conquered, overcome, and dominated by the thinking mind. In these frameworks, yoga, meditation, and the like are employed as tools for suppression. Yet when we develop the ability to focus and direct our attention, we no longer waste our energy on suppression. We no longer have to employ a warden to guard our jail because the door is open for anything and anyone to pass through. We are set free.

The state of orgasm is less about experiencing calm and more about meeting and welcoming whatever naturally arises. From this state, we are able to enjoy our lives, no matter the circumstances. We don't get hung up on suspicion or judgment, and so we can allow life to happen spontaneously, without having to stop it at the gate and run a security scan.

As we begin to embody this state, we notice that more occurs with less effort. When we're distracted by all of our need to make things happen, we're unable to be responsive. All of our bandwidth is occupied with the effort of trying to force our will. We become like Lucy and Ethel in the chocolate factory, struggling to keep up with all that's coming our way, but only becoming overwhelmed in the process.

Feeling overburdened, we declare it's "time for some self-care!" We need to relax! But instead of opening into orgasm and connecting with the energy that would truly restore our vitality, we unplug what's unplugged. We numb or dissociate, engaging in activities designed to turn down our feelings, whether it's binge-watching reality television, eating, eating, eating, exercising to exhaustion, or tossing back a glass of wine or three.

When we train to keep our attention on all that arises, we don't need to *recover* from life. We are enlivened by living. In the day-to-day, we are no longer wasting energy tolerating or trying to derail or oppose all that displeases us. Instead, we can accept it. It simply is.

In all of this we are directed by the wisdom of our desire—this evolutionary force that moves us in our own (and the world's) best interests. But it can be difficult to get there, because modern culture tells women that claiming ourselves means claiming our *independence*. That looks like demanding of ourselves that we be able to *do it all*. Somehow overwhelm has become a woman's birthright. To have the babies *and* be a good wife and mother *and* have a job *and* maintain a certain appearance *and* perform sexually in a certain way. All of our struggle is in claiming this self—this woman who is capable of doing it all without any help. We've lost our ability to ask for assistance, to engage with a community, yet we get angry that we're overwhelmed. But when you ask a *modern woman* what she deeply *wants* or what she *needs*, often she can't even articulate it, perhaps beyond saying, "I need more energy," or giving a list of complaints about what she *doesn't* want. This is what being fiercely independent has won us.

Like all great truths, there's a paradox at the heart of women's struggle. It is that when we sacrifice ourselves—when we release our personal will and our need for this form of independence—to desire, when we yield to its superior intelligence, we can finally *breathe out*. We are no longer gripping and clinging, trying to control everything. We can engage our will differently, as an energy that cocreates in concert with desire, but no longer seeks to control it. We allow our desire to possess us. This is what we truly long for.

So often we misunderstand our longing to be possessed. Feminists feel ashamed of wanting to be "taken," this desire having been projected onto a man, or men. This yearning to be overtaken that we feel is a yearning to release our control to the *energy of orgasm*. Yet because we feel this desire within our body, we think it's about sex. And because we have all these negative judgments about our sexuality, we feel ashamed. It, too, becomes part of our tumescence, and as such becomes distorted so that we can't see its true nature. And so we project our longing outward. There's nothing at all wrong with wanting to release yourself into sexual climax, but when that moment is done, we lose sight of our deeper desire to release ourselves into something larger and stronger than ourselves. This is part of how we conflate climax with orgasm—we mistakenly think our desire is about another person, or a brief experience. In reality, it is a desire to become *more of ourselves*.

I remember at one point, I was dating this man who I realized I didn't actually like that much, but the sex was really good. Through my OM practice, I had come to learn that my sex really belongs to me. It isn't another person doing it or creating those feelings. It's mine. It's my sex. It's my arousal. I had thought I didn't have access to these things and needed him to give me access. Turns out, I didn't need him for that. If I left him, I would still have access to those things.

As women, we're conditioned, and we condition ourselves, to look to men to unlock us. Then, if we have a great sexual experience, we think it's because of them instead of owning that it was inside us, all along. It goes back to the shame we have being sexual and owning our desire, regardless of someone else.

The path of reconnecting with our desire can be a challenging one. To truly become more of ourselves, we must accept all that comes with it.

Accepting the Mantle of Power

In Chapter 1, I described the difference between the princess and the queen. The first plays with power, often recklessly, while the second accepts the responsibility that accompanies true power. She gives herself to her role in an act of devotion, understanding that as queen, her will, for better or worse, will be done. And so she must be wise and thoughtful in how she directs her power.

We often bemoan the labors and trials of being a woman. Our sex, our body, our clitoris is the source of all our problems. After all, they're why we're kept down. And so we block ourselves from our power, because if we have no power, we are no threat. Maybe the world will leave us alone. But what we think of as trials are actually the gateway to our freedom, and the source of our power.

I will tell you—and having taken part as strokee or stroker in thousands of OM sessions, I can say this with certainty—that there is a spot on a woman's clitoris that, when stroked, opens a doorway to consciousness. All of her restlessness, her irritation, everything that is "wrong" comes from *not* being on this spot.

But when the lights are turned on inside her, a whole new sense organ engages. It is her Call.

Women have Call—even if we don't acknowledge it or aren't consciously aware of this power. But still, we have some sense of it. We use it all the time. We may have benefited from it. It's our untrained superpower. And without our awareness of it, or aware of just how powerful it is, we may shoot it here and there haphazardly, blowing a hole in the wall here, exploding a vase there. We send a man into a frenzy without understanding how deeply compelled he is to respond. Or sometimes we hide our Call so as not to attract attention or to, as we perceive it, cause trouble. Instead, if we want to become fully empowered, we must embrace it. We must wield it and become skillful at doing so, taking responsibility for how we direct it. We must own our Call.

A recent survey study of Call found that beneath the layers of social conditioning, there exists an innate, almost primal power in some women to consciously—or even unconsciously—magnetize others. Women who scored higher on the Call scale tended to exhibit more extraversion and were more receptive to new experiences and ideas. In essence, Call emerges not merely as a metric of sexual esteem but as an aspect of how we engage with life and the world around us.[41]

Typically, how we use our Call is by activating a man's biology. We attract him by being small, tightly contained, properly proportioned, well-manicured, helpless, and endlessly needy. But there are occasional signs of the monster that lurks below when we are irritable, controlling, critical, belittling, paranoid, or jealous. And he knows when we are not using our power for the greatest good. This is merely a distortion of power that has been caged, cut off from its wisdom.

41. Caroline Griggs and Rachel Pelletier, "The Female Power of Volitional Attraction: The Concept of Call," SSRN, February 7, 2025, https://doi.org/10.2139/ssrn.5128770.

When we reconnect *at a visceral level* with our disowned wanting, we can experience the deep healing that no amount of talk therapy can unleash. We come alive. Every aspect of us comes online, is plugged in. We embody our animal senses, walking into a room and feeling, hearing, *smelling* what everyone there wants or needs. And when we are responsible, when we are acting in concert with the energy of orgasm, we are generous in our response. We seek not to control others and/or to use this awareness to serve our own ends, but to serve *them*. To enliven *them*. For once a woman becomes truly free, she wants nothing more, or less, than for all others to be free as well.

Dr. Vivian Siegel at MIT, who conducted some of the research I referred to in Chapter 2 (finding that OM elicited a mystical state on par with the second-highest dose of psilocybin) says this about Call[42]:

> "I think one of the mysteries of woman, if you will, that people have puzzled over generations has been the power of a woman to attract, to influence, to invite armies, to destroy worlds, to create worlds. There are novels that have been written about this, poems, myths about women's power. I've heard from woman after woman who's developed a practice of OM that as she becomes more steeped in the practice, she starts to recognize that there's a kind of fledgling ability to communicate, to attract, to influence, to sway without words. Over time, they tell me that they learn to focus that ability. That's what we refer to as Call.
>
> "All science comes from noticing a phenomenon and wondering whether the experience is repeatable. Then, once you decide it is, you ask how it works. Any mother

42. Vivian Siegel, "Vivan on Call," virtual lecture, posted August 28, 2023, Vimeo, 08:41, https://vimeo.com/858770614/28def66930

knows that your heartbeat regulates your child's heartbeat. Any mother can tell you about a time their child was screaming and wailing with fever, and then she put the child to her chest and the child fell asleep. Anyone who's felt the effect of having someone they love hold their hand when they're scared has felt this.

"So we know about connection, and we know we crave it. We know how much something like a hug affects us. In many ways we're designed to connect to each other, physically, emotionally, psychologically, and through our nervous systems.

"I tend to think about Call the way I think about fire. There's this incredible force that is both creative and destructive. That is, to some degree, uncontrollable. If you can learn how to direct it, and use it in a way that chaos doesn't ensue, there's potential for enormous good."

To truly understand Call we must recognize that while a man's world is from the skin out, a woman's world is from the skin in. Deep inside, where she can access knowledge and nuance that men cannot even conceive of. (They have their own abilities.) A woman's nervous system is like a complex, multi-stringed instrument. When she unfreezes, she can play, and be played, with remarkable results. And she does not withhold her gifts.

Call functions in concert with *limbic resonance*—or the ability for humans and other mammals to share deep emotional states simply by being in close contact. As clinical psychologists Anthony Scioli and Henry Biller write in *Hope in the Age of Anxiety*, "Whenever two or more people come together, an emotional force field is created. If the emotions between them are ones of empowerment, intimacy, or reassurance, that field becomes a hopeful refuge. . . . [F]or example, the Elysian Fields were a blessed paradise where the bravest and most virtuous mortals would enjoy everlasting life and happiness. . . . [T]heir true locus may be in the here and now, between parents and their children, among friends and lovers, in secular as well as spiritual unions. Central to all of these attachments are psychic connection, love, and hope."[43]

From this framing, it is easy to see how limbic resonance provides a basis for healing. But it can be used in other ways as well. Consider how many successful men's careers or personal lives have been decimated simply because they could not resist the allure of Call.

As Peter Kingsley writes, "For the Greeks, Persuasion was, herself, a goddess—the archetypical power of the female at its most erotically alluring and seductive, a being of tremendous magic who is able to overcome all the force in the world."[44] As the saying goes, with great power comes great responsibility.[45] When we truly connect with our Call, others are at the mercy of how we feel, so a woman must develop the ability to direct her Call expertly, with generosity of spirit. She will need to examine all that she uses her Call for. To admit when she sends mixed signals. She will have to operate aboveboard, in plain view, rather than under the radar. She will no longer use her Call to curry favor or otherwise get what she wants. She will no longer manipulate. She will not need to, because she has become completely self-possessed and no longer relies on others to do her bidding. What she draws toward her naturally organizes for

43. Anthony Scioli, *Hope in the Age of Anxiety* (Oxford University Press, 2009).
44. Peter Kingsley, *Reality* (Catafalque Press, 2003).
45. "'With Great Power' - Marvel's Most Iconic Phrase," accessed January 27, 2025, https://blog.gocollect.com/with-great-power-marvels-most-iconic-phrase/

her benefit and her safety. At home in her power, her confidence confers power on others.

Women who live in orgasm do not play with their power like ignorant teenagers nor try to control others like the Queen of Hearts, ruling over Wonderland, proclaiming, "Off with their heads!" Living in orgasm, we live intimately connected to ourselves and those around us. We know exactly the impact we have on others, and its consequences, and we act with empathy and compassion. We know how to wield our power, and how to apply it at just the right time, in just the right manner, to empower others. This engaging of others builds relationships and breeds a healthy kind of interpersonal dependence. We learn to trust others as they learn that we are worthy of their trust. Who we show the world is who we are. There is no more need for hiding or deception.

At awards ceremonies, you often hear actors describing the *generosity* of other actors. Instead of trying to claim the best scenes or lines for themselves, they focus on how they can support their colleagues. They sense what is useful to the other actor and provide it, thus lending an additional energy and clarity to their performance. We can do this when we don't feel a need to stake out our claim—to demand that we're getting the best lines or enough screen time. We simply see the direction that energy or orgasm wants to move, and what wants to be enlivened, and we support it.

Now, everything I do in my job is orgasmic. I ask myself, "How am I the magic right now in this interaction? What am I here to say? What am I here to teach this person?" I ask for the ability to feel into them enough to know what's the next right thing to say or do. What's the next right stroke?

From this space, we are free to engage honestly. We no longer need to create boundaries nor patrol our borders because we know we can deal expertly with whatever appears. We are neither closed down nor completely permeable. We have the wisdom of semi-permeability, that can easily characterize the nature of anything that approaches us. Therefore, nothing is a threat.

Owning your Call is an essential aspect of living in orgasm. But this step requires courage, because Call is a massive power to wield. When we can channel our Call, we radiate a clear, direct signal that quite literally transmits sensation to others. That signal can be sexual in nature and it can create genital arousal, but it can be so many more things, as well. Directed to the spiritual body, the energy prompts presence. Directed to the creative body, it prompts inspiration. Directed to the emotional body, it prompts love. And we are happy to bestow these gifts because we have absolute security in ourselves and our place in the world. Our nervous system has become regulated, and so we can give and receive freely, no longer afraid to belong. To devote ourselves in service of love.

People may assume that those who live in orgasm only think about themselves and what they want to experience. But when a woman is truly connected with her orgasm, she brings out the best in those around her—emanating joy and possibility that is contagious to those around her. She sees in others what they are truly capable of—more than they can see in themselves— and draws it forth. When in a state of orgasm, we live in a state of interconnection where doing what feels good to us is beneficial to others.

There is a non-referential *rightness* to a woman in her true power. She does not look to others to tell her who she is because she *knows* who she is. She does not offer acts of generosity to gain acceptance, but rather, she does so because that's who she is.

Anaïs Nin once wrote that "Life shrinks or expands in proportion to one's courage."[46] To truly expand, to release all that now holds you back—those shackles of your own design—you must bring your most daring, bold, and adventurous self to bear. But the rewards for doing so are beyond your greatest imagining.

46. Anaïs Nin, *The Diary of Anais Nin*, Vol. 4: 1944–1947 (Harcourt, Brace & World, Inc., 1969), 125.

CHAPTER 5

What It Feels Like to Live in Orgasm

When we live in orgasm, we are, in a very real way, in every moment making love with life. We are bringing our full attention, curiosity, and energy to bear in cocreating reality. We learn to recognize life energy—the energy of orgasm—in all its forms, and we go *with it* in the direction it's guiding us. This is why living in orgasm feels like living in an ongoing flow state—we are flowing with the energy of creation.

In some ways it can be difficult to imagine what this is like because living in orgasm is a journey of discovery, of unfolding. Even the most skilled wordsmith is unable to impart the true taste of a delectable, fully ripe strawberry. To know what it tastes like, we must do the tasting. As Alfred Korzybski noted, "The map is not the territory." Or in the words of Robert A. Johnson, "We cannot say what joy is. We must go the further step and discover its true nature for ourselves."[47]

To know the experience, we must live the experience. At the same time, maps are incredibly helpful at getting us where we'd

47. Stella Resnick, *The Pleasure Zone: Why We Resist Good Feelings & How to Let Go and Be Happy* (Conari Press, 1997), 4.

like to go, so in that spirit, we can describe what it's like to live in orgasm. This conceptualization will also help you identify when you start to get that taste. But beware the temptation to overintellectualize. The mind can give us only one layer of understanding, but we have many more tools with which to perceive and communicate. Our nervous system is exquisitely wired to sense things far beyond our immediate, conscious awareness. For instance, our fascial system—part of the body's connective tissue network—has highly sensitive receptors that are constantly receiving and transmitting information at the somatic level. This is part of our system of interoception—our body's ability to sense what is happening inside us. But this is not just about us. We are connected to the world around us, and our bodies also process information we receive from sources outside our skin. Even our organs have highly tuned sensing and communication capabilities. And of course, there is the clitoris, which is the most magnificently sensitive area of a woman's body.

To inhabit this new territory and live in orgasm requires the body and all of its miraculous technology to come fully online. We must agree to venture into a space where we feel, at times, totally disoriented.

For one, understanding what it's like to live in orgasm requires that we dissolve our current, limited ideas of liberation, especially around our sexuality. For women especially, our sexuality is our expression of power into the world. Because so much of our power gets locked up in that. To understand true orgasm, we need to release the projections and definitions that have been placed on women's sexuality—whether wanton or chaste, for they live inside the same prison of thought.

Though sexual adventurousness can be a welcome result of finally throwing off the bondage of puritanical chastity, it can also be or become a reaction. The idea is not to ping-pong from one extreme to another, alternating in a cycle of binging and purging, but to get into a genuine relationship with your sexuality in a way that is true to yourself *as a woman*. That might look like throwing off the bondage and becoming really sexually adventurous for a while, because when you have been starving and finally start to eat, you realize the depths of how hungry you were. And, vice versa, it's possible to lose ourselves in the external validation that can come with sex, flexing our power and magnetism, but missing out on the deeper opportunity for full liberation by staying in that mode beyond its peak. We have the idea that we need to take on some fixed identity, either Madonna or whore, but what we're really looking for is the sweet spot that honors the relationship we have with our orgasm and our sexuality—their power and what they offer to us. The spot is dynamic, always changing, evolving, and we're learning to follow it to freedom.

One of the reasons women struggle with liberation is that we often lack a sense of our own self. While most spiritual traditions are designed to help men relieve themselves of an excess of self, women are chameleons, shifting based on our perception of the given situation. Functioning like this, we lack a frame of reference to transcend; there's no basis or foundation from which to move into the liberated state. We can't release because there's nothing to let go of. Unless we genuinely self-define and unleash, our accommodating nature will remain defined by the structures outside ourselves, our own desires and sight sublimated by what we think other people want.

As Riane Eisler writes in *Sacred Pleasure*, we presently live in a *dominator culture*, which operates through hierarchy and suppression. In contrast, the more egalitarian and communal *partnership culture* recognizes the wisdom and value of all members. Included in the latter is a deep recognition and appreciation for women's unique abilities to channel creative and life-giving energy. There is research that traces this cultural difference all the way back to the development of agriculture. First proposed by anthropologist and sociologist Ester Boserup,[48] cultures that farm using plows become male-dominated with a stark division of labor, since plows require men's upper-body strength. Cultures that farm using hoes allow for equal participation in agriculture. Data shows that even after industrialization, societies with a history of hoe-based agriculture tend to have more equitable gender roles, higher female labor-force participation, and more liberal views on women's roles.

In the West, we have evolved from agricultural, to industrial, to our new, post-industrial age, and we've watched the shift in culture progress in turn. Eisler describes her theory of cultural transformation, stating that when we experience periods of chaos—those where our social structures begin to disintegrate—a powerful opportunity presents itself for real social and ideological change. "However," she writes, "there is another possible outcome. This is for the dominator system to reconstitute itself in seemingly new institutional and ideological forms that merely co-opt some partnership elements while still preserving the same basic configuration that provides social and economic rewards for domination and conquest and idealizes, and even sacralizes, pain."[49]

We can celebrate the blockbuster success of *Barbie* all we want, but after the credits roll, the popcorn has been swept up off the floor, and the awards have been handed out, is our actual lived experience any different? Do we feel any deeper

48. Alberto Alesina, Paola Giuliano, and Nathan Nunn, "On the Origins of Gender Roles: Women and the Plough," Center for Economic Performance, November 2012, accessed January 7, 2025, https://cep.lse.ac.uk/seminarpapers/07-12-12-NN.pdf.
49. Riane Eisler, *Sacred Pleasure: Sex, Myth, and the Politics of the Body—New Paths to Power and Love*; (HarperOne, 1996), 177.

satisfaction or spiritual meaning in our lives, or do we still feel that we're constantly plodding uphill, struggling to assert ourselves . . . just, this time, wearing a lot of pink? Are we still trying to prove ourselves? To acknowledge our worth?

An Alternative Sexuality

When we live in orgasm, it's not necessarily about who, or how many partners, you're having sex with. Instead, we realize that in some manner, we are at all times making love with our life. We are engaged in a constant dance of creation, of which the sex act is one precious, powerful form.

This alternate paradigm is outside the action-reaction pendulum swing of wanton and chaste. Sexual adventurousness takes on whole new depths of meaning. It becomes an adventure in *intimacy*.

There is a step in Orgasmic Meditation called the "noticing," where the stroker briefly describes the strokee's genitals. They may notice the contours of the strokee's labia, or the color of her clitoral hood. For many strokees, this may be the most confronting step in the OM session, and we may be tempted to gloss over it or let our minds check out, rather than being fully present to these initial strokes of gentle, encompassing attention. But here we are practicing the feminine superpower of receptivity, allowing our stroker's words in, the impact of our own being on another expressed back to us through the lens of thoughtful attention.

We might wish to have more love in our lives and fantasize about how that might come to us, but then such an act of true attention is offered to us and we jump out of the experience. It can be confronting to be seen so fully.

By comparison, the world of conventions and transactions

can seem much easier—predictable, controllable. And if that is what you're looking for, then yes, it is easier.

> When I had my first OM session, it was in a room with others OMing. At first, I felt really embarrassed. It was hard to receive. I didn't like having all of that attention on me. After five minutes, I wanted to stop, but I decided to stay with it and just be present. I remember looking to either side of me where there was a woman here and a woman there, all lined up in our nests. It felt really good to have them near me, and then I felt myself dropping in. It still makes me feel emotional. It was like coming home. Like coming home to that place of truth, and we were all on that same journey, together.

When we live in orgasm, everything we do has a sense of possibility because we are living in flow. However, that doesn't mean life as we live it becomes *easy*.

Flow can show up in many different ways. During the Covid-19 pandemic, writer Lisa See was, like many of us, homebound. One day, while she was walking past her bookshelves, a title leapt out at her. She wasn't sure at first why she noticed this book, the cover being an unremarkable gray tone. Still, she pulled it out to take a look. It was a book about the development of medicine during the Qing dynasty in China. See realized that though she'd had the book for a decade, she had yet to read it. In her confinement, she figured there was no time like the present.

In that book, she learned about a woman doctor in the Ming dynasty who, in the year 1511, published a book of her medical cases. See looked up the book and discovered it had been translated into English. The following day, a copy arrived on her doorstep. The serendipities continued from here, including discovering that the woman who translated the original text just so happened to live 15 minutes away from See, and was happy to assist with her research.

The result was See's bestselling historical fiction novel, *Lady Tan's Circle of Women*.[50] That is one way living with flow can appear. Notice See did not create the thread. It was not an act of force or personal will that started her on the path and led her down it. She noticed the thread, then continued to follow. She said *yes*, and *yes*, and *yes*.

That's not the only way that living in life's flow can appear. There's a common myth in the personal development movement that says that when you are on the "right" path, everything will align for you, and that will look like ease. In reality, when we live in orgasm, we experience ease not because everything is easy, but because everything is *right*. We accept all that is.

That can look like writing a bestselling novel, or it can look like your house burning down. But in flow, we do not see those charred remains as an indication we have done something *wrong* or that we are on the wrong path. Instead, we see the rightness, the *perfection* that is present, even in what appears like a challenge.

Seventeenth-century Japanese poet Mizuta Masahide wrote:

Barn's burnt down —
now
I can see the moon.[51]

---

50. Lisa See, *Lady Tan's Circle of Women* (Scribner, 2023), Acknowledgements, Kindle.
51. Mezoff, Rebecca. "Barn Burned Down." Rebecca Mezoff Blog, August 25, 2013. https://rebeccamezoff.com/blog/2013/08/barn-burned-down.html.

This isn't some kind of magical thinking or convenient re-framing, it is answering *yes*. It is acknowledging and embracing life's superior intelligence.

To be clear, while the path opened for See in a way that seems outwardly pleasant or pleasing, she had to show up. There was a lot of work involved in birthing that book. Life did its share. See did hers.

Saying *yes* does not mean we're taken along for a ride. We are participants. We are not free of want and desire, but nor are we imprisoned by them. *Wanting* does not feel like lack. When we long for something, we can feel and acknowledge the tension it creates without labeling it as negative, or judging ourselves for not yet possessing the object of our desire. We do not ask ourselves what's wrong with us that we don't yet have what we want. Instead, we learn to luxuriate in the longing, under-standing that the tension it produces is a force we can harness to create.

Our desire is a dance with life. Our wanting points us in the direction life wishes us to move, and we learn to listen and re-spond. Like a ballroom dancer, we feel life's palm gently on our back, and with the lightest movement, we know just where to go. Life is a strong leader, and orgasm teaches us to remain in connection, guided by life's flow.

But the message our present culture would tell us is some-thing quite different. There is a masculine drive for rigid inde-pendence that claims following is weakness. That to be strong, women must lead the dance, assert ourselves, press our will. But what leads us? Notice there is no place in this model for us to recognize our desires, let alone be guided by them.

The more disconnected we are from our desire, the more tumescence is generated, blocking the flow in a cycle that re-inforces its freeze. If you ask a woman what she truly wants, many cannot even articulate it, we are so divorced from our desire. Consider, is there anything more terrifying than hearing our desire? Than listening to it? We employ countless methods to numb ourselves and silence the messages our body is giving us. We mute our wanting for so long, we become disconnected from our own sensing and intuition. It's why we stay stuck in the same cycles. Why we keep making the same mistakes and repeating the same dysfunctional patterns again and again.

We run from our desire, fearing where it may lead us. Fearing what we may become if we follow it.

When we live in orgasm, we learn to dive into the true depths of our desire. From above, it may appear incoherent, and our actions may seem impetuous or confusing. But beneath the roiling surface, the prevailing current becomes apparent, and the depths' stillness brings clarity. We are not removed from our life, but deeply situated within it, open and connected to the entirety of its expression.

We use our internal radar to navigate—to know when and how to move, our body sending and receiving signals, no longer blocked by tumescence. We recognize and are drawn automatically toward truth because our body is humming in resonance.

Having now integrated my past experiences into my system through OM, I can have different conversations with my patients than I ever could before. I don't even notice I'm doing it most of the time, it's just natural. I'm just open. That's because I'm living in orgasm.

I'll have them speak from their body instead of their head, and all of a sudden, they'll just start crying. They'll be so grateful that I took them there.

The other doctor who works with me will say, "You're so good at that." But I just know that it's what's necessary—that it's the thing that has to open up so they can access the gifts. The gifts of cancer. The gifts of illness. The gifts of trauma. It's these gifts that bring us out of our conditioning.

When we experience disease, it's so often linked to a kind of suppression of things that have gone unsaid or unacknowledged in our lives. It's like the disease is saying what we can't. When I see cancer, it's often like the body is weeping the tears that the eyes can't shed. When we live in orgasm, we open to full expression. It's not easy. Sometimes it's painful to say those things, or to acknowledge when we acted in ways we're not proud of, but the energy of orgasm helps us to work through all of that so we can release it into the flow and become reconnected with the whole of life.

Again, this doesn't mean that life becomes *easy*. We understand the value and purpose of what we might otherwise call hard. Thus, even the hard is welcome. We understand it is our attention—our love—that actually converts the uncomfortable into the desirable. It's like the fable, how the Beast transformed after Beauty saw his true nature. Her attention allowed him to reinhabit his princely self. Or perhaps it's more like *Shrek*, where Princess Fiona remained an ogre once the curse was broken. This was simply her in her perfection. When we live in concert with life's energy, we abandon pedantic concepts of good and bad, because everything belongs. We only need ask, "Does this serve my desire?"

The things we often avoid or judge—such as anger, force, and arousal—are, through our attention, converted into power, strength, stability, and intensity. From this space, we can welcome all that is, just as it is.

If we encounter a wild horse, we are neither frightened by it, nor do we feel the need to "break" it to gain control. Instead, we recognize there is a relationship we can develop. The horse consents to be ridden because it knows we will not try to dominate it, but that our mutual experience is made greater together. At times we may lead, or the horse may; there is no need to assert our will for its own sake. We *become* both the horse and the freedom, trusting and allowing ourselves to be directed by a force with greater wisdom than we, alone, could harness.

I grew up being dominated by physical violence and watching my mom endure domestic violence. When I became a parent at 35 years old, I needed a way to parent that did not dominate through physical force and violence. I was clear that I would not tolerate violence in my home. So as a new parent, I had to figure out how to be in relationship with my daughter as a human being whom I respected. This was the order and this was an adventure I embraced. I never wanted her to learn to tolerate violence from anyone—including me. This is the kind of divine knowing I get from Orgasmic Meditation.

Awakening Into Orgasm

Just as life in flow is not always easy, not every session of OM is bliss. To be sure, the return from numbness can be painful, like coming back in from the cold; numb fingers regaining sensation. Blood begins to flow, coursing through veins frozen in tumescence, bringing warmth to thaw nerves stiff from hibernation. When we begin to truly come alive within ourselves, the initial sensations may not feel like release, or relief.

When we first commit to our orgasm, either in the practice of OM or simply living in relationship with our desire, the sensations may be sharp. Fear, irritation, or hypersensitivity—it may suddenly feel like the volume has been turned up on all our senses. We've let go of the control that we have tried to force onto life, and it can feel terrifying because being seen means we no longer get to hide. Instead, we submit ourselves to the unflinching gaze that longs to see us as we are, in our perfection.

This is where we must go if we are to claim ourselves. We must welcome the gaze, be with the stroke, and notice all that arises within us. To notice our own unfolding. Our unfurling.

To awaken into orgasm is not like an ascension or a leveling up. It's an unbinding, allowing us to step into a more expansive version of ourselves.

We don't cut ourselves off from our life, we relate to it differently. We don't seek to destroy any other form of illusion or reality; we envelop it. All of reality, every form of it, is within you, just as everything in this world is within you. To be so big that you contain the cosmos, the Milky Way pouring out from us. To accept and embrace this largeness. To be fully unmasked. To see and feel and know that what you have inside you, what you offer the world, is sacred. To be in constant, willing cocreation with all of life, not only through sexual acts, but through *every* act that is life-affirming. That is what orgasm feels like.

Now you understand why, in OM, we talk of the need to train our nervous system. We have to broaden our bandwidth to be this kind of channel. To be able to welcome and see the perfection in all things.

Everything Is Beautiful

For a woman living in orgasm, there isn't any part of her experience she needs to exclude because she can see the beauty in everything, even pain. In the proper context, pain can be empowering. Enlivening. It can unlock things within us that were bound up tight. Trail runner Courtney Dauwalter describes how she savors what ultra-distance athletes call "the pain cave" because she knows this is a place where she can meet herself and expand her capacity.[52] "It feels like this is a special opportunity every time it arrives," she said.

When we live in orgasm, we see that everything is simply energy, which can be directed creatively and lovingly. This is not an exercise of our own will, it's an exercise in recognizing true beauty, already present. Just as the bodyworker's attention to our body supports the health that is already present within the cells, our attention supports the health that's already present all around us. It amplifies it, encourages it to become what it wants to become.

Again, our attention is powerful. It's essential that we truly understand this so we can wield our attention—our

---

52. Rebecca Byerly, "What Courtney Dauwalter Learned in the Pain Cave," *New York Times*, August 31, 2023, https://www.nytimes.com/2023/08/31/sports/courtney -dauwalter-ultramarathon.html.

power—responsibly. So we can direct our Call both wisely and skillfully. So we can step fully into our true role in the world.

It's not that a woman living in orgasm feels superior to anyone—being fully in the self dissolves the need for hierarchy. Steeped in her orgasm, she knows with absolute certainty that she has a role no one else can fill. Just as there is no part of her reality that she rejects, there is no question of her status or her worthiness in being perfectly, individually herself. When we live in orgasm, we come into relationship with everything around us, which naturally enlivens it, making even the most mundane come alive.

When we live in orgasm, we offer our attention without motive. We do it simply because it is our role to do so. Scientists have proven the existence of the *observer effect*, wherein the very act of noticing and attending actually impacts the state or behavior of the system being observed. Our attention is powerful. We impose no agenda onto the objects of our awareness. All that we wish is that everything we attend to, for every person we offer our attention, that they become more themselves. All that we wish is for others' liberation.

When we live in orgasm, we live in *perfection*, our natural state. In perfection, our whole self is in tune with the richness of life. We perceive the full measure of the world through our own bodies and feel an utterly rich and complete connection with all that is. We do not engage with the world from a motivation to fix a broken reality. We are instead able to sense life's wholeness and completion. There is nothing for us to, by force of will, *change*. The action we must take is to *allow*. We are an agent of flow, free to engage from a sense of wonder, curiosity, and awe. Instead of seeking to make things happen, we play with possibilities, observing what wants to unfold and supporting it with the energy of our attention.

In 2023, when Courtney Dauwalter took on three of the world's hardest ultra races in a single summer, it wasn't with an iron will and the determined goal to conquer them, it was with a spirit of curiosity and playfulness. She said she was excited to see what could happen.[53] Incidentally, she won all three—something no other runner, female or male, had ever done—breaking multiple course records in the process. Instead of following rigorous training guidelines, Dauwalter took an unconventional approach, eschewing strict regimens. Instead, she prefers to "tune in to my body and listen to it," allowing it to dictate what she does on a given day. She also ignores time goals during races and instead focuses on simply running and listening.

At times, we may confuse pain or difficulty for "punishment," believing if only we were somehow better, we wouldn't suffer. That judgment pulls us out of our body and into our mind and all its ideas about what is good and perfect. We chase perfectionism, trying to create perfection. Yet perfection cannot be created or even grasped, it simply is. Perfection includes everything, every part of ourselves, every experience, in a perfect whole. There's nothing we have to "do" but surrender to it.

When we ground ourselves in this perfection, we may still experience pain but discover that we are resilient. There's no need to avoid our experience. We go directly to the heart of our pain knowing that everything that happens in life, every aspect of it, is valid. Once we've seen through the veil, we are no longer limited. We are free to go wherever life takes us—to accept the invitation wherever it leads.

We can be in the pain cave because we do not see it as a bad place. It is merely a place. And as we spend more time in acceptance, we begin to see more often the humor that underlies this

53. Byerly, "Pain Cave."

experience of being human. As we laugh with life we see how humor increases the energy of flow. And not only can we accept and be present with pain and discomfort, we can also open to our own worthiness.

When we accept life's perfection, we experience a state of ease where we can release our judgments of wrongness—about others and ourselves. We can release our self-scolding because we recognize that our path simply *is*. We can recognize barriers to our own liberation without believing they are bad and shouldn't exist. That we should have done better. No matter—the opportunity is here now to make another choice, to take another path, to experience something else. To do so, we listen to what our bodies are telling us, and follow. And we develop an equal affinity for what we know, and what we do not yet know.

From this space, we no longer need to look to others for advice, to lead us, or to solve our problems for us. Instead of looking to the finite, we open to the wisdom of the infinite, understanding that flowing through us is everything necessary to dissolve the barriers to our liberation.

All of this capacity and awareness becomes available to us as we thaw and as our senses and everything they enable come fully alive. Reconnected with our senses, we naturally become aware of *excellence*—aware of beauty, meaning, sensory delight—even in what we would otherwise perceive as the ugliness and the despair of everyday life.

We do not need life to change so that we can feel good, because we see that everything is already good, already beautiful. And we see, too, that it may wish to grow. We recognize everything, including and especially ourselves, as perfect with room to evolve.

Reawakening the Senses

When we live in orgasm, we abandon the concept of the primacy of the mind and embrace the power of the senses. Today, we've become fascinated with neuroscience and isolating the brain's every mechanism because we believe that if we understand how our brain works, exactly, then we will understand how *we* work. The discoveries made by that entire field of science point to the truth that we can't fully isolate the mind from the body. The mind and body are intricately linked in their partnership through the nervous system. To attend to one and ignore the other keeps us trapped.

There is no primacy of the mind over the body, nor of the body over the mind. Instead, the two work in concert. When we allow each to serve its purpose, their dance together is elaborate and exquisite, allowing us access to our full capabilities. Therefore, as we awaken into orgasm, our first surrender is to release our consciousness to the body.

The realm of the body is foreign terrain to consciousness, the unknown geography where ancient cartographers marked their maps with dragons and other wild beasts of their imagination. Consciousness is most comfortable traveling its own liminal terrain; the groundless, unlimited space of the abstract. To consciousness, the body feels awkward, limited, even frustrating with its incessant concessions to materiality. That is why the mind prefers to restrict the body within its rules and expectations and beliefs—if it cannot be done away with entirely, at least the body can be controlled, its nagging desires and needs made predictable.

But there is something consciousness desires more than its relentless pursuit of dominance, and that is to be finally relieved of control, finally subsumed by forces more powerful, more intelligent, more intricately detailed and complex than itself. This is what brings the mind to the body, what has us surrender our own identity to finally be taken. This is the process of orgasm.

What we discover beyond the initial shock of being fully embodied is the expansiveness of our being. It is an entire universe waiting to be discovered and explored. It is comprised of its own physics, its own logic and rationale, which may seem strange and enigmatic to a mind that is used to simple theoretical frameworks, but in time we learn to trust the body and the felt language it speaks. Intuition streams from beyond horizons and depths we cannot fathom and yet its truth is there, laid bare for us to see. The famous Tibetan lama Chögyam Trungpa Rinpoche called this *crazy wisdom* because of how it appeared to those minds still hesitating on the shore. But for those of us in the ocean of direct experience, we discover that, "The crazy wisdom of directness, complete directness, involves relating directly with sanity, or bodhi mind."[54] No longer do we experience the world through the misshapen lenses of our preconceived ideas and abstract conceptual thinking. We dive into orgasm and feel the wetness for ourselves.

Despite what judgments may be cast upon us, we learn to play with everything, especially people's limited understanding. Our perspective and our compassion allow us even to love them for it. We understand that under our gaze, it, too, transforms. Softens. Moves into flow.

When we awaken into orgasm, we forget the belief that holds that women are weaker because of our incessant obsession with our *feelings*, which we so often judge as overwhelming or embarrassing. But once our consciousness has penetrated the surface

---

54. "The Crazy Wisdom of Directness," Chogyam Trungpa, accessed January 27, 2025, https://chogyamtrungpa.com/quotes/the-crazy-wisdom-of-directness.

level conceptuality of our emotions to their deeper experience, we discover they are composed of the sensations of the body and its desires. The ability to perceive these internal signals from the body is called "interoception," which science states is directly correlated with the ability to access the orgasmic state.[55]

Our feelings offer us a path inward, and it is our ability to follow the path that brings us toward our true power: the experience of our orgasm and all it calls into being. What we seek is not "out there" and never has been. As mythologist Joseph Campbell replied when asked why there wasn't a female version of the hero's journey, "Women don't need to make the journey. In the whole mythological journey, the woman is there. All she has to do is realize that she's the place that people are trying to get to."[56] Women, we are the destination. We are the goal, the jewel. We are the prize worth all the difficulties.

As we remember the jewel within, we become reacquainted with what has been dulled in us. In childhood, when we were shamed for our sexuality—as most of us were in some way—we learned to suppress it. But just like you can't dull only one emotion without dulling the others, women cannot suppress our sexuality without also muting the rest of our sensing. As a result, we lose connection with our intuition.

It can be challenging to regain—to re-enliven—our senses. As Stella Resnick writes in *The Pleasure Zone*, when we start to feel anything in the realm of pleasure—which is tied to deep sensing—it can trip a breaker in the fuse box and suddenly the system shuts down. We push back against it because we are

55. Ben Hall, "Interoception Enhances Female Sexual Satisfaction," *Neuroscience News*, Dec 11, 2024, https://neurosciencenews.com/interoception-female-orgasm-psychology-28231.

56. Sharon Blackie, "The Fairy-tale Heroine's Journey," The Art of Enchantment, with Dr. Sharon Blackie, March 6, 2024, https://sharonblackie.substack.com/p/the-heroines-journey.

unwilling to surrender to our senses. To be taken beyond the limitations of our logical, thinking self.

As Resnick explains, "Our pleasure-negative society, in both subtle and not-so-subtle ways, encourages us to seek pleasure outside ourselves—through consumerism, material gain, social validation, or passive diversions . . ."[57] For most of us, this pleasure aversion begins in childhood, when adults shame us or otherwise dampen our enthusiasm for life. As children, when we felt the urge to move, we moved! Only to be scolded by a teacher for not lining up properly for recess or smacked by a parent for fidgeting at the dinner table. We were taught to comply. As a result, Resnick writes, "We learn to restrain our natural need for physical affection, to be fearful of our sexuality, to withhold our exuberance, and to abandon our interests in favor of more practical endeavors."

As children, others suppressed us. As adults, we self-suppress. We internalize the programming, cutting ourselves off from the simple desires of the body and walling ourselves in with tumescence. This is how we become our own jailers. When we are pressed down in these ways—shown and told that we are too much or too little—our overall responsiveness to life becomes muted. We don't just self-limit pleasure, we self-limit *every-thing*. All our capacity to live, to experience vitality, becomes dammed up.

Forget about experiencing an expansive sexuality—we can't even allow time or attention to enjoy the full, luscious flavor of that deliciously ripe strawberry as it explodes on our tongues. Everything sends us into such overload, we cannot taste *life*. We lose the ability to deeply enjoy and metabolize everything from sex to a sunset to a sumptuous meal. We skate along the

57. Stella Resnick, *The Pleasure Zone: Why We Resist Good Feelings & How to Let Go and Be Happy* (Conari Press, 1997), 20-21.

surface, and so these life-affirming experiences never light up our cells in the way they could.

We feel cut off from life energy, because our *tolerance* for life is low. The smallest sip feels like drinking from a fire hose.

Resnick calls this limited capacity our *pleasure cap*—the point at which our system shuts down or begins to rebel. One of the most powerful ways OM transforms us is it alters our nervous system in such a way as to expand our capacity not just for pleasure, but for sensing overall. It enables us to be with everything. To be simultaneously aroused, or *turned on* by life, and also *grounded* enough to be fully present with it. Recall the scientific findings which demonstrate that OM increased the ability for people with a history of trauma to be with their arousal.[58]

As we awaken into this space, this way of being, this self-expansion into orgasm, we may initially feel an agitation or an irritation. That is primarily just the off-gassing from our tumescence. When we feel that, some part of us wants to stop, to shut down. But the solution is to stay with it and gently, slowly, go deeper. We may be at the edge of what our nervous system can process, and we don't try to push past that. Rather than trying to break through perceived barriers, we simply stay with each sensation—whether pleasurable or seemingly displeasurable—attending to it. Not trying to control it, stop it, or change it. Not trying to rationalize it or think it away, allowing it to soften in our nonjudgmental attention. In time, the body will open. Our capacity will expand.

When we live in orgasm, we stop turning to the mind to "solve" all our "problems." Instead, we light up the body's limbic system—the set of interconnected structures in the brain that, among other tasks, regulate our emotions. It is also one of the mechanisms that allows us to co-regulate with one another

58. Prause, "Effects of Adverse Childhood Experiences."

as we connect, interact, and affect one another on the emotional plane. The comfort we feel is expressed in our limbic neurology, our individual systems influencing one another. From this space of connection, and with the brain consciously online and engaged in service to the body, we can see the pure energy that is present. Our judgment that keeps us separate from our bodies—and each other—falls away.

We recognize that it is not a problem, it is simply an expression of tumescence. It is bound up and knotted and looks like a problem. But we sense into it, immerse ourselves within it. And it untangles. The energy is now free, liberated, and we can direct it toward creation. Our loving attention causes the knot to untangle itself. That's why complete strangers who stare into each other's eyes for several minutes almost inevitably start crying. Our attention has its own wisdom. It loosens one another's knots. We do not need to *do* anything.

When we awaken into orgasm, our perception feels stripped. Naked. Bare. Our awareness becomes a sea of vibrations. We are aware of heat. Of light. Of radiance. We see the dance of molecules behind objects we thought to be solid. And we feel a deep gentleness. The gentleness of life energy paying attention to *us*. Gazing into *our* eyes. And we feel *our* knots loosen.

We step into the flow.

As we look around, the perfection we observe in everything is not about a specific product or outcome or place or person. It is the perfection that always is when we are able to be fully present. Not just "quiet our thoughts" as we are told to do in typical meditation. But when we bring our body and all of our senses fully online. When we open to what we are shown. This is pure presence. Pure perfection. This moment.

Living in orgasm is about showing up fully, absolutely, in this moment. And this moment. And this . . .

CHAPTER 6

Female Orgasm
as a Spiritual Path

In the Sufi tradition, there's a fable in which the wise teacher Nasreddin is sitting in the middle of the marketplace, crying. His tears are of his own doing. He has a basket of peppers in front of him, and one by one, over and over, he reaches down, pulls out a pepper, places it in his mouth, and chews.

Finally, someone intervenes. "Teacher," they ask him, "what are you doing? Why do you keep eating those peppers when they are causing you so much pain?"

Nasreddin looks at the man through his watery gaze and says, simply, "I'm looking for a sweet one."

The story is straightforward; it's told as a cautionary tale about the dangers of desire. Following his yearning for a single sweet pepper, Nasreddin causes himself only suffering. If he could only disconnect from this desire, all would be well. Yet as psychiatrist and Buddhist scholar Mark Epstein underscores in his book, *Open to Desire: The Truth About What the Buddha Taught*, there is a second, deeper meaning to the fable.

Many spiritual stories center on young monks or other novices learning key insights. But Nasreddin is not new to this game.

The situation is quite the opposite—he is the teacher. So, what wisdom is Nasreddin imparting on us? As Epstein frames it, "Like it or not, he is saying, desire will not leave us alone. There is hopefulness to the human spirit that will just not accept no for an answer. Desire keeps us going, even as it takes us for a ride."[59]

Conventional religion and spirituality would have us believe desire and pleasure are anathema to spiritual development. If only desire would leave us alone and we could master our detachment, we'd alleviate suffering. But that long-held belief is a common misperception. Ironically, the idea that desire is bad and to be avoided causes much more suffering than desire itself. It's our attempts at renunciation that have disconnected us from life, causing such great pain.

Epstein goes on to explain that the Buddha himself realized after a time that austerities would not unlock enlightenment—they would simply kill him. By starving himself, he might rid himself of the needs of the body, but he would also die in the process. By closing himself off to desire—not only his desire for food but for pleasure in all forms—he would be cutting off all access to life energy. That's all well and good if your goal is to depart the physical form entirely, but while we're human beings in an embodied form, we need to feed—both literally and figuratively—those human forms.

Oftentimes spiritual and religious pursuit is spurred by a hope to be rid of the endless cycle of desire. We hate ourselves for our desire. We struggle with it. Suppress it. But it's the *ignorant* view of desire—the clinging or gripping, the refusal to let life move and flow—that causes suffering. So if a masculine path of spirituality restricts itself to abstinence, rejection, and austerity, the feminine path dives into the deep end where we

59. Mark Epstein, *Open to Desire: The Truth About What the Buddha Taught* (Penguin, 2005), 2.

must learn to unleash our desire. Released from the chains, we are free to be taken by the rapturous flow.

> I've seen among my patients that if they're part of a religion or spirituality that emphasizes men or subservience to men, it's like they are getting an extra dose of that message. We all get it from the culture, and then if you're in a religion that says this, it reinforces the message even further. This can make it even harder for women to connect with their own desire, and to speak for themselves from that space.
>
> Each of our desires is so different. What I desire is different from what you desire, or from what he or she desires. And that's why it's so important to connect with our desire, because it guides us to our purpose. When we suppress desire, as so much religion does, it cuts us off from that, and that leads to disconnection from life, which leads to disease.
>
> When women start to connect with themselves, it's literally like a light comes on, and it starts to shine. But so many don't even know what they want, and so they can't have the life they want. When you start recognizing and following that desire, it's like a flower that starts to blossom.

OM teaches us to work *with* desire instead of against it. And indeed, even Buddhism considers desire to be the most powerful energy we can engage for our enlightenment, with practices reserved for the highest practitioners of secret "Tantric" initiations. As the Indian guru Sri Nisargadatta once declared, "The problem is not desire. It's that your desires are too small."[60] If we stop desire short of where it would eventually take us, it's like walking out of the movie only halfway through, complaining that none of the storylines were resolved. By allowing desire to be our guide and follow it truly, we will ultimately discover what we've longed for.

Letting our desire lead us is not the same as being a slave to desire, or to endlessly seeking pleasure. It is not about reserving our "yes" for only what feels pleasant. Instead, our desire informs us. We welcome pleasure, and we also welcome what does not feel so wonderful, accepting that all that arises is good in that it has been called in to serve our desire for our own evolution.

We are often too quick to label the experiences desire delivers to us, preferring to identify *what* it is instead of remaining with the mystery long enough for its gifts to be revealed. Buddhists use the word *emptiness* (or *sunyata* in Sanskrit) to point to the *absence* of those labels from the mystical unfolding that is ultimate reality. Yes, reality is entirely lacking the names, conceptions, and judgments that we associate with our everyday world, but absent those fixed and finite forms is not nothingness—it is total fullness of possibility. It is complete abundance, all potentials ready to be realized. It is the realization that nothing, on its own, has any nature inherent to itself. Nothing is disconnected or independent. Everything is revealed as more complex than our ability to conceive.[61]

When we see this, we are released from our unending struggle to make sense of things or distinguish this from that, good

---

60. Epstein, *Open to Desire*, 8.
61. Rod Meade Sperry, "Understanding Emptiness — in 50 Words or Less," *Lion's Roar*, February 17, 2016, https://www.lionsroar.com/understanding-emptiness-in-50-words-or-less.

from bad. Instead, we see an equal preciousness to all people and the entire infinity of things down to the most minute, incredible detail. As Buddhist philosopher Nagarjuna said, "Thanks to emptiness, everything is possible."[62] And OM is the fastest, most effective practice to help us see this for ourselves.

This is why we say orgasm is a spiritual path. It is a path of personal development where we seek to recognize not only our own perfection, but the perfection in all things. When we live in orgasm, our natural aim is to operate for the highest benefit of all. To get there, we learn to harness the sexual impulse, and ride it all the way to our own awakening.

Healing the Separation of Body and Mind

Eros—the *erotic*—is that which yearns for connection. It is the animating force of life, the drive to union, to creation. Our sexual impulse is that life force made manifest on this plane of existence and is our most direct path to the divine. Orgasm is our body's direct experience of that sacred energy. As we recognize the erotic impulse of our own body and being as an instinct toward the sacred, as we baptize ourselves in the completeness of orgasm, we begin to recognize the sacredness in all things.

Eros is the universal life force that fuels all existence. It is the raw, dynamic vitality that flows through the body, the mind, and the spaces between people, shaping experience, creativity, and connection.

---

62. Thich Nhat Hahn, "The Heart Sutra: the Fullness of Emptiness," *Lion's Roar*, September 16, 2022, https://www.lionsroar.com/the-fullness-of-emptiness.

This energy is neither created nor destroyed—only accessed, directed, and then liberated through intentional practice. When allowed to flow freely, it fuels expansion and presence, promoting our ability to move through life with ease. However, when blocked or suppressed, it can solidify and stagnate into tumescence, manifesting as frustration and resistance

Orgasmic Meditation serves as a direct pathway to engaging with and refining this energy. By focusing attention on sensation, OM practitioners learn to channel and amplify their energetic awareness, transforming raw life force into heightened states of clarity and interconnectedness.

Look around you. See the sun cresting behind the mountains and dispelling the cold of night. Look at the butterfly as it alights from the flower to land briefly on your hand, then flutters away. Gaze at the delight in a child's eyes when they awaken from sleep to see their mother. The sacred is not rare. But *recognizing* the sacred requires communion. It requires engagement. These things exist in every moment, all around us, but we overlook them. We dismiss them as banal, pedestrian. It is our attention and appreciation that elevates them. That elevates *us*. And again, this attention—this ability to *fully attend* to the world around us—is what we train through the practice of OM. And it requires that a transformation take place within us.

My spiritual path really started when I started OM. I never thought about meditation or anything like that prior to that point. I wouldn't have even been able to sit still long enough to meditate. I was always on a mission! I knew there was a voice inside that I listened to and that I trusted, but I wasn't on a path.

At the same time, I had always been interested in sexuality, even as a teenager. I was reading about how so many women can't have orgasms and wondered, *Why is that? Why would a woman fake an orgasm?*

When I eventually became involved with the OM community, I realized it's actually a spiritual path. It was like so many things were opening up, and I was experiencing the world differently. OM brought me closer to my sexuality, and that brought me closer to this spiritual energy. I started to see how we're all connected, and how what I do and say, and how I am in my life, impacts the world.

When I'm getting ready to see patients, I sit there and I think about the magic that wants to come in. I have that vision and that question in my mind: What magic wants to come through today? What's the thing that each person needs to hear or to see? Part of that is the ability to sense resonance. Through stroking, we learn to feel resonance. And with my patients, when the magic is coming through, if it's the right thing, I can feel that resonance with their body saying, "Yes, this is what I need." It's a mystical experience because you're listening and being led—that's orgasm.

Connecting to orgasm requires the mind to surrender to the body at a fundamental level. When this happens, the mind begins to ask the body, perhaps for the first time, "What is it that you want? What do you desire?" It's a stark shift for the mind and its assumed supreme position over anything as lowly as the material body. But as the body responds, we begin to realize what all of our objectification and neglect and domination have done to the body. How they have diminished the body and how that shapes a destructive way of perceiving the world. When the mind yields to the body, a new mind blossoms—a resilient mind that knows how to open, absorb, and convert every experience to love.

When we open fully to desire, we move beyond deprivation or craving. Instead, we relate to our wanting, our longing, with a view similar to that of the Sufis—we hold an understanding that all longing is really our wish to connect with the divine (whether that be God, Source, the animating force of nature, or however you characterize that which organizes or animates life). It also represents the divine's wish to know us. (It's not surprising given this view of longing and desire that Sufis commonly refer to the relationship with the divine as one between lover and beloved.)

Our desire doesn't merely symbolize our yearning to connect with all that is, it is also a tool we can use to do it. It is what draws the mind into the body. Any approach that prizes the mind over the body supports a harmful disconnect that only enhances our feelings of separateness from the world, because what we are cultivating is a separateness from ourselves.

OM seeks to heal this separation. It restores the connection between body and mind, recognizing the inherent wisdom within the body. It is an intentional practice in which we work with our attention in an optimal state of arousal, engaging both body and mind together. Instead of sitting on a cushion alone, sitting still with our eyes closed, we are training our attention in conjunction with signals received and processed through the body, while in connection with another.

Instead of transcending the world of matter, seeking to be apart from it, OM invites us in. Masculine spirituality is based on ascending above matter; feminine spirituality is a multidirectional expansion. It creates a deeper joining with the world around us. This is how we learn to be with all that arises.

From this space, there is nothing we need to escape. What we are transcending is our own judgments. Our resentments. We transcend our withholding.

Instead of fear or judgment, we engage with curiosity. We aren't looking to "tolerate," straining our ability to be with whatever arises. In orgasm, we engage in the anticipation of whatever is coming, expansive in the possibility of what it may be.

Our joy is boundless; it is not conditioned on *the right thing* coming into being. Instead, we recognize that if it comes into being, then it is the right thing. And we recognize that this is not a space we arrive in once, but one we return to over and over again as we relearn to live seated in the domain that is our birthright—orgasm.

The Path of Refinement

When we practice OM, we harness the sexual impulse within a time-boundaried, safe container for the purpose of training our attention. It is a practice of *attending*, for both the strokee and the stroker, and thus we learn to attend to life.

Over time, our attention becomes less pointed. Less angular or poky. Less about coming from a particular part of us. We begin to attend to life through our self as a whole. We are multi-sensate.

We describe this state as being "lit up." Unlike a flashlight, which emits light in a directed beam, we become like a star or a firefly radiating light in all directions. Our attention becomes *ambient*. We do not perceive or relate to things directly, but rather we inhabit the medium of attention. If something is present in the space, we are aware of it. And we can affect it. This doesn't necessarily look like trying to do something with or to it; we can affect it through presence. Through resonance. For instance, if we *are love*, we are emanating love, and that love can initiate a state change in others, or in the environment around us.

In OM, when we speak of refinement, it is the idea that we are always seeking to evolve. Yet at the same time, we recognize that who we are or where we are is *good* in and of itself. That's what we mean when we say, "Perfect, with room to evolve." We continue to hone our awareness, becoming more and more skillful in how we relate to life.

Peak performance is a term that's commonly used today, and we typically understand it from a masculine perspective, in terms of productivity. From the feminine approach, we might think of our goal instead as *peak oneness*. Or perhaps, *peak connectedness*. We lock into the vow of a bodhisattva—to get out of suffering, the causes of suffering, and get others out of suffering. Or the orgasm version: get into flourishing, the causes of flourishing, and get others into flourishing.

Mastery in OM is not about attaining some static state of having been there and done that. We recognize that enlightenment is a moving target. That's not discouraging or frustrating; it's liberating. We become free from the idea of achievement. We drop out of the ultramarathon of striving.

Perpetual refinement is not hierarchical, like unlocking the next level in a video game. And *mastery* is not about becoming forever unstuck. Instead, it's about having the wisdom to know how to meet the stuckness when it inevitably arises. Integrating it as part of the wholeness. It's about developing the understanding and awareness of what tumescence is, and what it feels like, so we can convert it on an ongoing basis, each time we encounter it.

Eventually, we become so skillful in this process that it becomes habituated. Knowing that liberating what's stuck releases our vitality and makes energy available to us, we begin to actively seek out that which feels difficult or unfamiliar. When we encounter it, we don't have to consciously deploy our tools anymore; it all becomes second nature.

Part of this process is to learn to stop gripping. Recall that at the start of this chapter I explained a different interpretation of what causes human suffering. It is not desire, but rather our impulse to cling to our idea of what we want or to try to force it to happen. When we do this, we interfere with life's flow. We create tumescence.

In the physical practice of OM, we learn that gripping dulls sensation. As we are stroked, a feeling arises that we like. We want more of it. But the stroke changes! We become frustrated. We want that feeling back! We begin to chase it, thus ensuring that it will not return, because even if it intended to return, we wouldn't recognize it. Our very chasing numbs us to the sensations we are actually having, rendering us incapable of feeling. We cannot flow from this space.

The same is true for the stroker, who may experience a sensation as pleasurable and try to hold onto this state or "make" more of it, disconnected from what the spot is actually asking for, thus numbing their own sensitivity. And so we learn to release our grip. This is how in OM we practice non-attachment. We observe the sensations and let them rise and pass, much like watching waves at the ocean. From this space of non-judgment, we do not castigate ourselves when we notice our own gripping. Recognizing our grasping or any unconscious habit is not a failure of practice; it's exactly where we can choose freedom.

When we live in orgasm, we recognize that in every experience there is something to be learned. So we engage our curiosity. We ask, *How can I offer love even to my penchant to grip?* The answer is that the urge to grip points us to recognize the absence of bliss and, from there, its restoration.

Consider an example outside the OM nest. Perhaps there's something you desire in your life. A fulfilling relationship, a new job, or a child. Then, you get it! The object of your desire materializes and your inclination, because you desired it *so much*, is to hold onto it with all your might. Yet doing so renders you *unskillful*. You may become jealous with your partner, perfectionistic and overbearing at work, or a helicopter parent monitoring your child's every move.

Gripping is like compressing soft tissue—unrelenting pressure flushes the life blood right out of the area, and the tissue becomes stuck, adhered, necrotic. But when you release the pressure—when you release your jealousy, your compulsion, your controlling—the blood rushes back in. Health is restored, and you can now see the difference between what happens when you smother and control versus when you allow life to flow.

This awareness is trained in the OM nest. We notice a pleasurable sensation, and we grip it. We notice our gripping, and we release it. When we relax, all feels new and exhilarating.

Similarly, we learn to release our avoidance or judgment of "bad" strokes—the ones that do not feel pleasurable. Through refinement, we quickly recognize our own judgment and love even it, thereby liberating any energy that was trapped there. In so doing, we recognize that even a "bad" stroke offers us something good—even if what it offers is the opportunity to recognize what we would prefer and ask for that adjustment from our stroker. Or we may recognize that along with our dislike of a stroke is a certain curiosity for what may lie beyond our preference, and we can choose to explore where we would normally disconnect. There may be something worth obtaining in the undesirable, and thus it becomes in its own way desirable.

When a monk leaves the monastery or the ashram, he doesn't leave his teachings behind. He relates to the world outside those walls *as a monk*. Similarly, when we leave the OM nest, we apply what we have learned there to all of life. We interact with the world as someone who is *turned on*—who is living in orgasm. As someone for whom sexuality and spirituality, body and mind, are linked.

OM and Awe

As neuroscientist Andrew Newberg explains in his book, *Sex, God, and the Brain: How Sexual Pleasure Gave Birth to Religion and a Whole Lot More*, OM creates similar patterns in the brain as other meditative practices. Newberg writes, "[T]hese findings directly link sexuality and spirituality as the changes observed during the OM practice much more represent other spiritual practices rather than sexual excitement itself. In particular, decreased activity observed during OM was in areas that are part of the default mode network which is active during the resting state of the brain and has been shown to be decreased in other meditation practices."[63]

While the default mode network (DMN) isn't bad—for one, it's largely responsible for those *ah-ha!* breakthroughs we have when we finally solve a problem that's been plaguing

---

63. Newberg, *Sex, God, and the Brain*, 78.

us—when it's overactive it can create negative feeling states. Conversely, quieting the DMN also quiets our ego. It mutes our self-criticism, our anxiety and worry, and even diminishes feelings of depression.[64]

Another experience that's linked with decreased activity in the DMN, and that can arise during OM, is feelings of *awe*. As psychologist and awe researcher Dacher Keltner defines it, awe is when we encounter the sensation of a vast mystery that transcends our understanding of the world. Awe shares characteristics with *flow*, including a sense of timelessness and connection with all that is. And like flow, awe is something we definitely want more of in our lives. As research shows, not only does it engender feelings of humility and being connected with something greater than ourselves, it's also linked with compassion, kindness, and relationships. It makes us feel more satisfied with life and causes us to care more about others. It decreases our sense of personal entitlement—makes us act more morally, and exercise more generosity. Experiences of awe have also been shown to increase our mental and emotional well-being.

Yet awe isn't just one thing. Keltner and his team isolated eight distinct types of awe, including spiritual awe, or a sense of connection with divinity. However, the most common source of awe isn't found in a church or even gazing at a sunset—it comes from other people. It comes from what Keltner calls moral beauty. This includes witnessing acts of love from one person to another. This can be an act of sacrifice on behalf of a stranger or a family member. It can also include the wonder of direct, deep, and sustained connection with another person, such as the kind we experience in OM. But there's an adjacent

---

64. Dacher Keltner, *Awe: The New Science of Everyday Wonder and How It Can Transform Your Life* (Penguin, 2023).

category as well, which Keltner explains, in which people describe a kind of sexual awe.

Orgasmic Meditation, because it's a contained practice of connection coupled with the power of sexual energy, provides us multiple paths to awe. We have a sense of being one with our experience in OM.

When a stroker and strokee attune to the same spot, they experience a shared interconnectedness and from there, an intimacy with all that is. When we leave the nest, this intimacy of spiritual awakening is felt by the world. We radiate it like the glow of the moon.

Saturated in Orgasm

In our awakening, we do not lose our sense of self, as is so commonly associated with classic ideas of transcendence—that up-and-out state of leaving the body behind. Instead, we become more deeply *rooted* in ourselves. Rooted in life.

Our consciousness expands. Our connections deepen. Our awareness becomes so broad it encompasses all that is. We envelop the universe, welcoming it within us. We connect with the sacred and the divine within and outside of our self. We connect with a Self that is larger than us, but also within us.

This is orgasm in its *saturated* state. It is more intense, more encompassing, more lasting than any material climax could ever be. That is because orgasm has become liberated from our genitals and is something we experience with our entire body. Through OM, we learn to distribute our sensitivity through the whole of our nervous system. This diffuse, simultaneous, and nonlocalized expression is the very nature of the feminine—it is a woman's awakening.

When we practice exclusively masculine forms of liberation, we experience only partial freedom. In feminine liberation, we "surrender into," instead of "separating from." This body-based state in which we radiate and resonate with all that is consumes us completely. It is only in this space that we experience true liberation. We no longer look "up there" or "out there" for guidance. We need look no farther than the here and now. Everything around us informs and directs us, and we are able to perceive these messages because our senses have become so open and highly tuned to life.

From this place of radical connection springs spontaneous compassion. Our generosity is ignited. We embrace every challenge that appears, asking, "How can I love even this?" We learn to respond instead of react, understanding that impulsive reactions cause us to lose ourselves. Responding, on the other hand, is skillful—both intuitive and thoughtful.

As Indian philosopher J. K. Krishnamurti explained:

"If you watch, looking out of the window and not saying a word to yourself—which does not mean you suppress the word—just observing without activity of the brain rushing in, there you have the clue, there you have the key. When the old brain does not respond, there is a quality of the new brain coming into being. You can observe the mountains, the river, the valleys, the shadows, the lovely trees, and the marvelous clouds full of light beyond the mountains—you can look without a word, without comparing."[65]

This is how external circumstances lose their control over us. The movie *Rosewater* tells the story of journalist and film-

65. From the outline, p. 134

maker Maziar Bahari, who was wrongfully accused by the Iranian government of communicating with an American spy. While he is in Iran reporting on protests against the country's presidential election, Bahari is taken captive and imprisoned. Over a period of 118 days, he is tortured and interrogated.

At one point, Bahari sits in his cell, wrapped in utter despair. Then, he gets word from his fiancée, who is pregnant. His baby is going to be a girl. In an instant, his world shifts. His perception changes. *A girl!* Suddenly he is swimming in the current that flows through all of life, and it transforms him. His mind is flooded with the strains of Leonard Cohen's "Dance Me to the End of Love." As if hearing love's call, he rises and begins to dance. He realizes that his captor cannot own him. Cannot overpower him. Despite his confinement, he has been set free.

It is as Richard Lovelace writes in his classic poem, "To Althea, from Prison":

"Stone Walls do not a Prison make,
Nor Iron bars a Cage;
Minds innocent and quiet take
That for an Hermitage.
If I have freedom in my Love,
And in my soul am free,
Angels alone that soar above,
Enjoy such Liberty."[66]

Mark Epstein writes, "Desire is the crucible in which the self is formed."[67] In this poignant scene, we see how Bahari's love for his family is more powerful than the circumstances that

---

66. Richard Lovelace, "To Althea, From Prison," Poetry Foundation, https://www. poetryfoundation.org/poems/44657/to-althea-from-prison
67. Epstein, *Open to Desire*, 9.

surround him. Prison walls cannot contain his love for his new baby girl, his joy at her existence in the world. His love connects him with a truth that is greater than his perceived imprisonment. He becomes larger than the prison. Engulfs his jailor. As he *becomes love*, in that moment he can love even that which seeks to oppress him.

Yet as women, perhaps the greater challenge has been to love *ourselves*.

A Woman's Awakening

Women have been saddled with so much projection, and our bodies the focal point of so much criticism, we have not only experienced a separation of body and mind, but also body and self. Through OM, this, too, is healed as we recognize the inherent goodness of our physicality.

In being stroked, in staying present with all that arises, in releasing into a greater sense of true self, we become witness to our depth of beauty. During the practice of OM, we realize that our bodies, which have been so misunderstood, seen as the source of our misery, are actually the source of our awakening. We recognize the clitoris—this most sensitive part of our bodies with its 8,000 nerve endings—as being exquisitely designed to make us sensitive to the world, to stimulate our unfolding. In a very real sense, *we were made for this*.

To this point, we have experienced life with its pain and adversity as something to escape. Our understanding begins to evolve, to alchemize, and we instead begin to turn toward our discomfort. Toward our emotions. We let go of dissociation as a coping mechanism. There is no longer anywhere else we wish to be.

The most beautiful aspect of OM is it speaks this sweet

wisdom to women through our bodies. No longer do we have to run. To hide. Now we, too, can be here, now.

It is safe to come home.

We also understand that we are both transcendent and immanent. We do not need to learn the secret code. We do not need a go-between, or an interpreter. We can access everything through our body, and through the body of nature. We *are* the body of nature, and nature is inherent in our body. In each and every moment, we are in harmonious creation with life.

An awakened self is a whole self in every moment. No longer do we put on masks or inhabit various roles depending on the situation. We are our full self in every encounter, in every moment. Instead of chasing life, we draw life toward us, into us. Everything becomes imbued with meaning and beauty, because we recognize in all of life the impulse that animates.

From this awakened self, we can create without exhaustion. We are fueled by the act of creating. In the Western approach, gestation, birth, and child nurturing are characterized as draining. Depleting. In Chinese medicine, birth and postpartum are recognized as an opportunity for the mother to strengthen her life essence and significantly improve her long-term health.[68] The act of creating and nurturing doesn't exhaust the mother; when it is attended to properly—when *she* is attended to properly—it fuels her. Women in the Western world sometimes describe gestation and birth as tearing them apart or ruining their body. Chinese medicine recognizes the extreme *openness* of these processes, both literally and figuratively, and it sees the positive aspects of this opening. It understands that we can be

---

68. Laura Stropes, L.Ac., "'Sitting the Month' - Chinese Postpartum Resting Month & Herbal Soup Recipe," Mayway, https://www.mayway.com/articles/chinese-postpartum -resting-month-and-herbal-soup-recipe.

broken open to life, and in our healing, become stronger and more supple than we were before.

In OM, we give birth to ourselves and in the process are blown open. To *stay open* is to live in orgasm.

Having liberated our energy from tumescence, we create ourselves by how we choose to invest this energy. We direct our attention thoughtfully, heartfully, merging with our environment. It is a truer, deeper kind of presence than any other kind of meditation can enable.

Gone are the distinctions between do-er and done-to. Gone is any kind of artificial separation. We feel in our bodies the truth that there is something of the other in the self, and something of the self in the other. We become intimate not only with ourselves, or with a beloved, but with all of life.

Pema Chödrön once observed, "Although we have the potential to experience the freedom of a butterfly, we mysteriously prefer the small fearful cocoon of the ego."[69] When we live in our tolerating mind, where we engage with life in limited and conditional ways, our mind is consumed with difficulties. We are so focused on struggle that our mind can scarcely take the time to relax and receive what is truly there.

OM splits open our cocoon. We emerge into the world, ready to welcome it all, from the profound to the profane.

The special purview of the spiritually actualized adult is to love the unlovable. In this space, we become privy to the unlovable's secrets. This is how we learn to turn poison to medicine, and this becomes our directive. To convert the smog into oxygen. And we do this through the only medium that's capable of such a task—our body.

---

69. Pema Chödrön, *The Places that Scare You* (Shambhala, 2018).

CHAPTER 7

How Orgasm Enables
True Equality

Women's liberation as we have known it is not an actual movement. It's not a collective action. It's a *reaction*. And whenever we react, we are locked into a doomed dance with whatever incited our pushback.

True freedom can only come from action that is independent of the structure from which we wish to break away. In other words, we must *create something new*. And to create something new, we must be able to envision something new. For women, when it comes to true equality, to true freedom, to true liberation, that new way of being will come about when we recognize what has always been true; when we embrace the wisdom and the power that has always been available to us.

In our very cells, in our bones, we are made to be conduits of power. We are *already* conduits of power. The problem is we've either ignored this fact or run from it. When we have sought liberation, instead of turning inward, we have looked out—to men, and to the masculine structures society inhabits. We have decried those structures as our oppressors. But it's like we've been "locked" inside a room with only three walls, standing there shouting at the door and demanding to be let out when we could simply turn and see that we're not actually imprisoned.

Yes, it's true that in a masculine power structure, women are confined and restricted, that we have to shoehorn ourselves in, compress and deny pieces of ourselves. That these structures do not serve women. But how we've gone about changing that is all wrong. Instead of insisting the men change the masculine structure so that we may better work within it, we must step outside of it entirely. We must relate to life in an entirely different way. That sounds like a tall order, but in reality, it's simply a return to our own true nature.

In the mainstream medical system, there's this sort of code that practitioners follow. Instead of being able to *go there*, meaning to tell a patient what you think would truly change their situation, or instead of being able to guide them to that place, there's a protocol. It's like, if someone is prediabetic, my inclination is to recommend dietary changes to prevent it from happening. But instead, I'm supposed to prescribe a treatment. If you have cancer, there's a treatment protocol that involves chemotherapy and radiation. If you have high cholesterol or asthma, there's a treatment. But I've actually cured people's asthma without a dose of drugs.

When we're connected to ourselves and our deep intuition, we can operate beyond these rigid structures. We—women and men—can function beyond these algorithms and connect with what's truly needed in each situation—what the body truly wants in order to not just mask or alleviate symptoms, but to actually heal.

Even as doctors, mostly we don't think for ourselves. We don't read the literature to understand that cancer comes from malfunctioning mitochondria, and that's what should inform our treatment—supporting the body's natural systems. Instead, we get these directives from drug manufacturers.

It's like with our food system. We're all programmed to operate within this system where companies that make processed food want us to eat junk and sugar, and that's preventing us from healing. They're all part of these controlling structures that don't orient toward health or toward thriving. But if we can learn to turn inward, we'll hear the messages our body is telling us about what's good for us. About what our bodies desire, and that includes what actually nourishes us.

This works on all levels, so when we do this as individuals—when each woman becomes liberated—it will contribute to a liberated society.

When we live in orgasm, we develop the tools to inhabit ourselves and life fully—the awareness, the focus, the stamina, the self-confidence. When we live in orgasm, we stop performing the role of "woman," and instead actually become one. This means we stop abiding by—whether by conforming to or rebelling against—masculine definitions of what and who a woman is. Rather, we allow what is inside us to fully blossom. Instead of trying to be the moon that reflects a male sun, we shine with a light of our own, then let the rest of life organize around us.

True women's liberation is not a response or a pushback,

it is a dissolving of all the externally projected definitions and self-defining from the inside out.

The Two Queens

When we are truly liberated, we become like a center of gravity around which an entire solar system organizes. When a woman comes into herself, men "fall in line." We commonly misunderstand what this phrase actually means. We think it means to yield to a superior power, when it is simply a natural response when a powerful organizing principle makes itself known. This is the way of all nature. It is not subservience or acquiescence, but an understanding of place and order. Of where and how we all fit.

By now, most of us know the story of the wolves of Yellowstone. Fearing the predators, we killed or otherwise removed all of the wolves so the other animals in the park might thrive, with disastrous results. A tremendous imbalance in flora and fauna resulted, with bodies of water actually changing their course. When the wolves were reintroduced, all fell back into balance.[70]

Women are like these absent wolves. As a result, our systems have fallen into disarray. In the absence of women's willingness to carry the mantle of true power, men have self-organized into power systems that destroy rather than support our various ecosystems, which function more as ego-systems.

The return of Woman—our full and rich engagement—is necessary to restore balance, to provide a true, benevolent power source to which men can orient.

If you read that with a mind oriented toward the masculine, that might sound controlling or manipulative, but it is anything but. Consider again the idea of the queen in balance—the

70. "How Wolves Change Rivers," posted February 13, 2014, by Sustainable Human, YouTube, 4:33, https://www.youtube.com/watch?v=ysa5OBhXz-Q.

Benevolent Queen—versus Wonderland's Queen of Hearts. The latter is the domineering leader who works within the masculine structure, who plays power games by dominating or deferring. But the Benevolent Queen is not concerned with making or coercing anyone to do anything. Instead, she is interested only in playing her role, in inhabiting herself fully. When she stands firmly in herself, everyone else knows where to stand. They have a sense of belonging. They know their place—not in a hierarchical sense, but in a eudaimonic one—where each of us can live richly and fully according to what brings us the greatest sense of meaning and purpose. According to what most enables us to flow with life. This compassionate queen who is at home in her own authority is not the realm of a select few—it is the rite of all women. It is the space we naturally evolve into as we open into orgasm.

Although the Queen of Hearts rules with an iron fist, there is actually a power gap. In the vacuum created by a lack of women who fully acknowledge and follow their own desire, men go hungry. If there is no queen who is worthy of admiration, no queen that men wish to please, their own highest identity is left unfulfilled. There is no quest to fulfill.

In reflecting on the current state of dating, mathematical physicist Eric Weinstein recounts a conversation with a woman describing her phone as the "singles' bar in her pocket." She feels terrible that this is what her exchanges with men have come to—swiping left or right—yet she feels she has no other choice. Weinstein reflects on the larger impact of this commodification of dating and sex by apps that reduce interactions to mere preludes to sex.[71] "I don't think it's a good deal for young

71. Tom Bilyeu, "Society is a Ponzi Scheme," February 23, 2022, posted March 21, 2024, by Tom Bilyeu, YouTube, https://www.youtube.com/watch?v=18bhyZIFXF4&t=903s.

women at all," Weinstein tells the interviewer. "I think that young women have been used to putting men through their paces and demanding a lot, saying, 'Jump this high,' and seeing who can clear the bar. When that power is not present and when men can't win these competitions and have these competitions really mean something, we derange the society."

It doesn't simply boil down to sex (at least not the actual sex act), but to the fact that women need to live in a place where simply being who they are inspires men to great acts. This isn't about a barroom brawl to see who can impress the girl with their strength or a competition to see who can make the most money (though all of that behavior has very real roots in our biology). That's all a distorted view of male-female dynamics. Instead, because women have never truly embodied our power—or at least not in any way or at any time that we can easily recall—we must look to mythology for a better model. To legends such as King Arthur and the Knights of the Round Table, who operated by a code that, at its heart, was in service of women. Or to India's epic *Mahabharata* and the story of the Pandava brothers, who waged an entire war to protect the honor of pure creation itself—as represented by their shared wife, Draupadi. These challenges weren't simply to impress a woman or win her favor, they are what caused them to become *better men*. Chivalry isn't about holding doors, it was a system of values to which a man could orient his entire life.

This is a natural yearning for men—to want to have a woman so centered in her own power that she brings out the best in him. How many masculine proclamations of love and devotion have hinged on this very desire: "You make me want to be a better man."

The Queen of Hearts requires compliance. The Benevolent Queen inspires those around her to discover and inhabit the highest versions of themselves by doing so herself.

A woman seated in her power reigns. She doesn't need others to love or worship her, nor does she require their protection. She is not self-reliant, but self-possessed. She understands that reliance on others is not a bad thing; it is the interweaving of the fabric of life. Threads alone will fall apart. Together, they make a tapestry.

In a powerful woman's presence, men are no longer just doing, they are *doing* in alignment. Their actions have a deeper value. In the presence of a woman in her power, a man does not need to be directed; he self-organizes to his own greatness. But instead, women have been playing small.

As Clarissa Pinkola Estés writes in *Women Who Run with the Wolves*, women have been in hiding, living "desert lives: very small on the surface, and enormous under the ground."[72] Life sustains itself in the desert, but no trees can grow tall. Instead, vegetation stays close to the ground because it lacks the abundant resources necessary to unfurl. Women need to keep these desert roots—to stay deeply grounded. But we need to abandon the space of scarcity where we believe the only resources available to us are those that men—or anyone we perceive to be in power—will give us, or that we can steal. We need to move on from the finite game.

Opening to Infinity

Up until now, our collective concept of liberation has looked like the flip side of what we have always had. Like switching stereotypes from being defined by culture as "subjugated" to being defined by culture as "liberated." Yet within this we are still masculinizing the feminine. We have moved *beyond* nothing; we

72. Clarissa Pinkola Estés, *Women Who Run with the Wolves: Myths and Stories of the Wild Woman Archetype* (Ballantine: 1992), 36.

merely inhabit another role inside the same restrictive framework. We are still buying into masculine values.

Again, when we act in *response* to a form, we continue to power the form. Even in our denial or rejection, our fighting or separating, the old form still works through us. Triggered by our boss or our beau or our brother or our father, we think, "I'll show him!" Thus, anything we do from that point forward is a response to the initial male impulse or action. We must de-link ourselves from this system.

When we react to masculine constructs, we think we've changed the paradigm, though we've merely shifted from checkers to chess. But they're both played on the same board.

Fighting the powers that be is a method learned from the powers that be. The same is true for the very belief there is anything to fight. Spiritual writer and translator Mirabai Starr writes that when St. Francis heard the call from Jesus to "go and rebuild my church," he didn't set out to take on the entire Catholic establishment. Instead, he created something different—a new movement that was not a response to what he believed was lacking in Catholicism, or where the Church was going astray. He created something based on his own vision and understanding, a movement powered by the life energy moving through him. St. Francis, who felt himself deeply rooted in nature, wasn't a rebel—though some have characterized him as such—because he didn't push back on the Church. He merely lived *better* and let his life and his actions demonstrate the love that he believed was the true essence of his relationship with God.

We waste our time fighting against masculine constructs. When we struggle against them, we are only prolonging their demise. Instead, we must focus on building a new way that renders the present one obviously obsolete. Obviously inferior. When we define the new and build accordingly, we withdraw our energy from the old systems. When women step into our power, it will become so evident how much better—how much richer, how much more fulfilling, how in line with love—this way of being is that the other will hasten to fall.

The building we must undertake is building ourselves. It is establishing our own identity. This is a woman's work. For too long we have adopted masculine spiritual concepts that work only for men. They are centered on self-negation and denial, like ice baths and water fasting. These do not work for feminine realization.

As Clarissa Pinkola Estés writes, Baba Yaga—the mythological witch who in part represents women's deep, wild nature and mystical powers—cannot sustain herself on cigarettes and lettuce.[73] She must *eat*. She must nourish herself.

According to spiritual writer Caroline Myss, St. Teresa of Avila was renowned not only for her deep love of God (there are many accounts of her levitating while in the throes of spiritual ecstasy), but she also had a deep love of food. She enjoyed cooking and consuming it.[74] She loved to sing and dance and play music. Even though she took vows and lived a life removed from everyday society, instead of renouncing all pleasures, the Carmelite nun was still very much of this world. She lived richly, but not because she was without care. Not because she wasn't paying attention or had no woes. In fact, she suffered painful physical afflictions for most of her life. But she did not seek to be delivered from this world; instead, she embraced it. She developed a rich inner life, then inspired those around her as she embodied the love she experienced. Myss writes, "Teresa explodes the myth about mystics that, once God has called you,

73. Estés, *Women Who Run with the Wolves.*
74. Carolyn Myss, "Entering the Castle," Myss.com, accessed January 28, 2025, https://www.myss.com/entering-the-castle/st-teresa.

your life becomes one of suffering and poverty. In her case, and in other cases like that of the great Sufi mystic Rumi, God consumed Teresa and Teresa consumed God . . ."[75]

Women do not need to extinguish our appetite, our hunger, our desire, our power. We need to develop, evolve, and come to know them. We do not need to preoccupy ourselves with selfless acts so we may be deemed good enough. We have no self to begin with. We do not need to renounce or deny our bodies when our bodies have never been our own. Instead, we need to claim them.

> Orgasm helps every woman reclaim herself. As I've seen in my practice, a huge part of this is reclaiming her voice. It's connecting with her innate truth—no matter how unappealing or scary it might feel—and expressing it, first to herself, then to others.
>
> In the couple I was working with where the wife had bladder cancer, I realized that whenever she was asked a question, she took a long time to speak. In that space, people—including her husband—often jumped in and filled in her answers. She was not speaking for herself. When we created a space where she could speak, that's when she was finally able to express to her husband that for essentially their whole marriage, she hadn't felt like she'd consented to sex.
>
> Up until that point she'd been holding it in, and it had been blocking her "turn on"—her ability to connect with the aliveness of life. She was cut off.

---

75. Myss, "Entering the Castle."

All of this was hard for her husband to hear, which of course makes sense. So I turned to him and explained how good it feels to have someone be a full-body *yes* with us, and how I wanted that for him. He liked the sound of that, so he was able to drop his own defenses and be present with what she needed to say.

I just kept asking her questions about what lights her up about life. It was hard for her, but finally she said, "Horses." So, we went a little further, asking more questions. And then the tears came. That was her releasing grief. And we held the space and just let her feel that. And after that she did something I'd rarely seen her do—she smiled. Over and over, that's what happens. If we can let ourselves be with the grief, feel it, process it, then the joy can come through. And so I sort of coached her husband on how to be in that space with her where she can do that, so he was also learning how to relate not just to his wife, but to relate to life differently.

This is how a woman's opening benefits everyone.

It is similar to Mesopotamian goddess Inanna, who journeyed to the underworld. She left her culturally rooted self behind and discovered a richer, truer identity. Through this action, this walking away from social constructs of her own selfhood, she became the queen of all worlds.

Thus, women will change the system not by trying to change men, but by donning our own crown. In this we must make the shift to see that a woman's power is her appetite. Her ability to draw others—to draw the world—to her is her gift, and it is her purpose. In this evolution, or involution, is the recognition of what constitutes power, and what constitutes force. When we perceive the difference, we relate to the whole of life differently.

As physician and psychiatrist David R. Hawkins writes in *Power vs. Force: The Hidden Determinants of Human Behavior*:

"[F]rom time immemorial, man has tried to make sense of the enormous complexity and frequent unpredictability of human behavior. A multitude of systems has been constructed to try to make that which is incomprehensible comprehensible. To 'make sense' has ordinarily meant to be definable in terms that are linear: logical and rational. But the process, and therefore the experience, of life itself, is organic—that is to say, nonlinear by definition. This is the source of man's inescapable intellectual frustration."[76]

This is the realm of the feminine—what is organic, ever-changing, and endlessly interrelated. What is confounding, moving, and defies easy explanations or oversimplification. The feminine embraces the ever-evolving infinite. Masculine approaches lose sight of the whole by capturing static images and trying to tease them apart through endless separation and reduction. The feminine can perceive the whole because she does not rely only on her rational mind. To perceive the whole involves using the body as a satellite dish to take in the signals and arrange them into meaning.

Hawkins writes, "We can intuit, then, an infinite domain of infinite potential—consciousness itself—which there is an enormously powerful attractor Field organizing all of human behavior into what is innate to its 'humanness.'" This power of

76. David R. Hawkins, *Power vs. Force: The Hidden Determinants of Human Behavior* (Hay House, 2002) 70-71.

attraction—of magnetism—is what women transmit. When we step into it, society will self-organize around us.

In the absence of the feminine aspects of understanding, we have constructed rigid rules. We have been bound within what historian and religious scholar James P. Carse calls the "finite game," the goal of which is to win. In this shift, we move off the checkerboard into the infinite game, the goal of which is endless play. As Carse writes, "Finite players play within boundaries. Infinite players play with boundaries."[77]

There's this aspect of OM that opens us to true experiences of equality. I remember early on, the man I was partnered with was white, and something inside me really pushed back against that. Like, if I let this man stroke me it was like this white man owning me. But when he actually sat down next to me in the nest, that dissolved. Suddenly, he was just human. It was like everything inside me was shifting. I can still cry just thinking about that. It was like it broke down all of these ideas of separation that I had growing up as a poor kid in the Bronx.

When you live in orgasm, you become more inclusive and more inviting—of other people and of just life in general. You can just love people, period, without all of these divisions.

It's like, what is the degree of damage that has to happen inside a person for them to stand there and watch someone be hanged from a tree? What is the pain you're going through that you can inflict so much pain

---

77. James P. Carse, *Finite and Infinite Games: A Vision of Life as Play and Possibility* (Free Press, 1986).

on others, or watch it be done? What is the pain that causes that kind of rage, or hate, or numbness? You see those things, and you recognize the degree of damage that must have taken place inside someone for that to happen. With OM, we turn inside and connect with those things inside ourselves, recognizing that we all have some kind of tumescence. And we liberate that tumescence and share that liberation with the world.

In my own life, I feel this sense of openness and confidence that I never had before. I don't have that feeling like I need to hide. I don't feel weighed down. I operate on a deeper level.

There's also a freedom in my thinking where I can be with whatever is happening. It's a kind of grace. When I moved a little while ago, I wasn't sure if I'd like living in a different state. But afterward, I recognized that feeling that my home is inside. I'm at home, period.

In the finite game, we endlessly affirm our ego. We stake out our space. We seek to capture power. In the infinite game, we dissolve into orgasm. Instead of being endlessly concerned with our rights and our declarations, we let the power moving through us do its own work. We radiate true beauty rather than try to simulate and reflect a culturally endorsed idea of beauty. Instead of *acting* free, we *are* free. Instead of playing at power or trying to look powerful, we live in our power.

Being Consciously in Power

To be clear, women are always in our power. It is impossible for us not to be because we are made of it. If we are conscious inside our power, it can have aim; it can be directed. If we are unconscious, it is directed by whatever our default settings are, which are usually plugged into female cultural conditioning, our habits, the things we avoid and things we grasp for. We work to "own our man," but we also play the innocent. It is exhausting.

Power moves through women in ways that are either unskilled or skillful, but it is always moving. It holds men down or empowers them. One of these things is happening at all times because a woman's power is always moving.

And it is a natural truth that men are responders to power. In this way, an unconscious woman is a danger. We might as well yell to her, "Hey, watch where you point that thing!"

This is why women must make conscious our desire, despite what we think of it. Whether we label it as pretty or ugly, as refined or ribald. The fact is women often want things that culture might characterize as lewd, bawdy, wicked, or simply raw. We want to take a too-large bite and feel the juice running down our jaw, and there is nothing wrong or bad about that. Just as power moves through women, women's desire always exists. It cannot be shut off. It can be driven underground, and largely has been, yet that only means that a woman will experience her desire as something happening *to* her. But a woman who owns the full spectrum of her desire—who can meet it as it is without judgment and with full approval—is a powerful force, indeed.

This means we do not get to parse our desire as acceptable or not acceptable. We must rubber-stamp it all: *Approved!* We cannot do this wholesale, meaning we must be aware of each of our desires so we can interact with it intelligently. But we do not get to negotiate with it.

To identify our desires, we may have to dig for them. Like those desert roots, they may be so deep underground that they are not easily located. When we do find them, even if they seem unpalatable or inconvenient (perhaps especially if they seem so) we must claim them.

When a woman finally rises up fully in her power, she becomes naturally generous. No longer is she preoccupied with getting her fair share. She realizes the shares, as such, are hers to give, and there is plenty to go around. Finally, men can receive the power they have long hungered for and have been trying to manufacture themselves.

And yet, many women still struggle to even say the word "power," let alone embrace it. They will dance around with polite terms, like "empowerment." But this keeps actual power at arm's length. It says, "I'm afraid of you."

Largely, women fear power because those women who have expressed it have done so through their bodies, as this is the source of women's power. And look what happened to them . . . The acrid smell of burning flesh still hangs in the air. This is the dilemma of women's power.

Yet there is no withdrawing from the game. If we attempt to do so, life will again and again present us with situations where we have the opportunity to shed our tumescence. It will invite us over and over to live in orgasm. This can look like suffering. Like experiences we do not want to have. But if we instead choose the path of opening, we can learn to become conscious of power as it moves through us. Beyond awareness, we then begin to bypass hurt, tears, and rage, as they become unnecessary. We can move directly into creativity. We learn to direct our power.

The practice of OM has taught me to tune in to myself and to the present moment. Orgasm allows me to notice how much I love my life. I have learned to open and experience life rather than just thinking about life. I have become receptive in places I was not able to receive light and love and generosity.

I am able to sense hidden, unexpressed pockets of pain and joy in my patients and guide them to put attention there. Then I watch them release tension, tears, and rage, followed by joy and levity. Afterward, they become grateful for the gentle but direct attention. That is when my heart sings because my attention landed on the spot that wanted to be freed.

How OM Helps Us Embody Our Power

In the OM nest, we ask ourselves again and again, "How can I meet this stroke in such a way that there's resonance?" We don't wait for the "right" stroke; we learn to attune ourselves to the stroke that is happening. Then in life outside the nest, we don't wait for the right things to happen before we opt to join in. We don't reject what arises. Instead, we attune ourselves to what is happening. We ride the wave that is emerging.

Through the practice of OM, we learn that the least important aspect of our experience is the *content* of what's happening. That represents a shift from the finite to the infinite game, where we are limited by narrow interpretations of occurrences—this is "good" and this is "bad"—and instead ask, "How can I meet this in such a way that there's resonance?" "How would I respond, seated in my power, capacity, and worth?" And when things feel especially challenging, "How can I love *even this*?" There is no doubt it's possible, we simply must locate that resonant tone.

The more we are willing to meet life on its terms, remaining open to things as they are without needing to try to change them or wish for them to be a certain way, the more our lives become characterized by the state of being in orgasm. We are ever in a state of arousal, meaning we are ready to meet and integrate whatever comes. Our fire burns hot enough. Our consciousness has become strong, supple, responsive, and open enough to handle the situation, and we know this.

As long as we meet life with this kind of receptivity, as long as we meet others with this kind of receptivity, no person or situation can ever have control over us. Suppression is an illusion—one we can cast off at will. But instead of pressing back against it, we interact with it skillfully. We release the tumescent energy of the situation and direct it into creating something different.

In this space, everything belongs. We therefore learn what it *truly* means to belong—not only to one another, but to life. There is no longer aloneness, no longer a sense of disconnection. We radiate connection, and love, and the world around us reverberates with this frequency.

Gandhi called this interrelationship "the divine mystery supreme." As he said:

"We but mirror the world. All the tendencies present in the outer world are to be found in the world of our body. If we could change ourselves, the tendencies in the world would also change. As man changes his own nature, so does the attitude of the world change towards him. This is the divine mystery supreme. A wonderful thing it is and the source of our happiness. We need not wait to see what others do."[78]

This is what it means to belong to the world. To belong to our own heart. To belong to our own body.
And when we belong, nothing in life is off-limits.
This is true liberation.
This is unconditional freedom.

78. "Be The Change," Genesisca, accessed January 28, 2025, https://www.genesisca.org/single-post/2019/06/17/be-the-change.

Acknowledgments

For my sister, Iris—My first best friend, my fiercest protector, my forever heart.

For my daughter, Sheniqua Donesa Rattler Diaz—My one and only. It took me fifteen years, science, and the grace of God to bring you into this world. You are the dream I refused to stop dreaming.

For Lasha Pierce, MD—My sister, my comrade, my heart. Every time I struggled to single parent my child while becoming a doctor, I would remember your strength and tell myself: If Lasha could do it with three, I can do it with one.

For Nicole Daedone—Whose courage, brilliance, and devotion to truth lit the path for me. Telling the truth about women's power—about Eros, about pleasure, about what it means to be fully alive—comes at a cost in this world. And still—you went first.

For Kenton Samuels—Since 2018, I have loved this man who shows up every single day, not with grand gestures, but with steady hands, a soft heart, and a quiet, relentless devotion that never lets go. Thank you for loving me home.

For Heidi Hudson—My ride-or-die, my travel buddy, my best friend. Thank you for being my yes—to travel, to life, to friendship, to joy. I am forever grateful.

For Every Woman—May she find her people—the ones who love her whole.

—Teresa

From the Author

—Nicole Daedone

I want to know life biblically, the way a man knows a woman, the way a lover knows a beloved. I want to know the water by getting wet. Theory, commandments, and concepts leave me hollow. My driving questions when I come across dicta and dogma are, Is that true? Is it wholly true? Where and how is it true? For whom is it true and why? Can it withstand the test of time? Is it true for me as a woman? The last one has taken me off many a beaten path. Givens are often no longer givens when I ask this question. The world turns upside down. As a free woman, I want all things to be free, liberated from any ideas I would impose on them.

We are constructed of the divine. I believe everything—and I mean everything—when properly tended to, reveals an untold beauty. But my work is not as activist, reformer, saint, teacher, guru, or shaman—it is as artist. Erotic artist. The art I do is akin to found-object art: art made from what has been thrown away. It's an art that turns something back into itself. Like turning prisons into monasteries; the unconscious realm of sex into the spiritual plane of Eros; the degradation of addiction into the art of addiction that isolates the addiction drive for purposes of realization; the life sentence of trauma into human flourishing; the feminism of subjugated women into the feminine collective of inestimable power; those who have been canceled, exiled, and banished into the leaders of the next era; desertified soil into not only carbon-absorbing but nutrient-producing; hunger and food deserts into farm-to-table, free, pop-up restaurants; black culture into the black box for society that holds the secrets. These programs exist, and you can find them here: www.unconditionalfreedom.org.

I founded OneTaste to reawaken our connection with intimacy, with each other, and to the primal source of energy that drives our creativity—sexuality. I created a contemplative discipline around Orgasmic Meditation (OM) that offers an immediate experience of what happens when we unleash rather than repress who we are. Since then, we have gathered some of the greatest research psychologists and neuroscientists to study the intersection of sexuality and human potential, in the largest study of its kind since Masters and Johnson. We know that OM has perhaps the most powerful effect of any natural process on healing trauma, promoting well-being, and transcendental experience. I have gathered people and created systems so that the vision can be manifested and grounded in observable benefit.

My work remains as it always was: to turn poison into medicine and make it available to those who want it. But for those who need it, here is the conventional side of things: I graduated from San Francisco State University with a degree in semantics and gender communication. I cofounded the popular avant-garde art gallery, 111 Minna Gallery, in San Francisco's SoMa district, before founding OneTaste.

I have appeared on *ABC News Nightline*, and my work has been featured in *The New York Times*, *New York Post*, *San Fran-*

cisco *Chronicle*, and *7x7* magazine, among others. I've written for *Tricycle: The Buddhist Review* and I wrote the book *Slow Sex: The Art and Craft of the Female Orgasm* (Hachette, 2011). My 2011 TEDxSF talk on OM has been viewed over a million times on YouTube.com.

About the Author

—Dr. Teresa Diaz

D r. Teresa Diaz is a physician, healer, and rebel heart who believes menopause is not the beginning of the end—but the beginning of becoming. Trained as an OB/GYN and now practicing functional medicine under the banner of Orgasmic Medicine, she offers women a radically embodied approach to aging, vitality, and erotic aliveness.

Born into poverty, racism, and trauma, Dr. Diaz navigated physical violence, sexual abuse, loss, and the crushing weight of perfectionism before discovering that healing is not about control—it's about reclamation. She lost over 140 pounds, healed from lung cancer after declining both chemo and radiation, transformed her health, rebuilt her life from trauma, and dared to reimagine medicine not as symptom suppression but as soul restoration.

Her work bridges science and spirit, clinic and kitchen table, hormone therapy and Orgasmic Meditation. She helps women decode the language of their bodies—sleep, weight, libido, rage, tears—and translate it into power. Her method blends bioidentical hormones, lab-based insights, plant-based nutrition, trauma healing, and the sacred art of desire as compass.

A student of Nicole Daedone and longtime practitioner of OM, Dr. Diaz teaches that Eros is not a luxury. It is life force. It is medicine. It is the pulse of the woman who remembers that she was never broken—only waiting to come home to herself.

About Soulmaker Press

Soulmaker Press is an independent publisher whose books span the fields of feminine spirituality, liberation, social justice, women's power, flow consciousness, and more. Soulmaking—a concept drawn from James Hillman's work on connecting life and the soul—drives our mission. The house publishes print and eBooks, pamphlets and chapbooks, podcasts and audiobooks, as well as a newspaper and other occasional material.

Soulmaker Press is committed to the dissemination of Erotic Philosophy, also referred to as Eros, the path of feminine spirituality. Eros is a force of creativity, genius, and connectivity. It animates and unifies the physical and tactile, saturates our experiences, draws us into engagement with other humans and nature, and grounds us in the deepest core of the soul. There is a special interest in the shadow, the unconscious, the creative process, and a feminine nonrational system of order.

The company's work is inspired by the five-volume collection of *The Eros Sutras* written by Nicole Daedone, the founder of Orgasmic Meditation. *The Sutras* are the essential texts in the study of Eros. Four of the five volumes have been published, with the final volume, *Liberation & Justice*, slated for release Fall 2025.

Since 2022, Soulmaker Press has published 13 books, including four national bestsellers, several of which are now available in public libraries. Six additional works are slated for publication in 2025. Our publishing history has been shaped by distinguished collaborators, including Ira Silverberg, co-founder of High Risk Books; David Ord, former Editorial Director of Namaste Publishing; and Beth Wareham, editor of several *New York Times* bestsellers.

Resources

Also by Nicole Daedone

The Eros Sutras, Volume 1: Principles

The Eros Sutras, Volume 2: Tumescence

The Eros Sutras, Volume 3: Orgasmic Meditation

The Eros Sutras, Volume 4: Relationship

The Eros Sutras Workbook, Volume 1: Principles
with Aubrey Fuller

The Age of Eros: A Manifesto of Connectivity and Consciousness

Erotic Justice: Making Social Change from Love

Play: A Path to Genius

The Art of Addiction: Re-Envisioning Addiction's Role in Our Lives
with Kate Feigin

The Art of Soulmaking: A Path to Unconditional Freedom
with Beth Wareham

The Art of Soulmaking for the Incarcerated
with Beth Wareham

From Guards to Guardians: Rebuilding Prisons from the Ground Up

The Erotic View on Trauma (mini eBook)

Slow Sex: The Art and Craft of the Female Orgasm

Other Resources

Sex, God, and the Brain: How Sexual Pleasure Gave Birth to Religion and a Whole Lot More by Dr. Andrew Newberg

For courses and additional information on Eros and Orgasmic Meditation, visit: **www.ErosPlatform.com**

For more on the science of Orgasmic Meditation, visit: **www.IOMFoundation.org**

For more from Dr. Teresa Diaz, visit: **www.OrgasmicMedicine.com**